UNDERWATER WORLD PUBLICATIONS LTD

A contemporary engraving of the wreck of the 'Brazen', showing the clifftop apparatus used to haul to safety the lone survivor (see chapter six).

KENDALL McDONALD

Great British Wrecks

VOL. THREE OF THE WRECK DIVER'S LOGBOOK
PART OF THE DIVER GUIDE SERIES

40 Grays Inn Road
London WC1X 8LR

Cover picture: the wreck of the *Brazen* by Ted Shipsey.

Book designed and edited
by John Hall

Maps and production by Suzanne Blyskal

Typeset in Times by P&M Typesetting Ltd,
Linacre House, Southernhay East, Exeter EX1 1UG,
and printed by Adlard & Son Ltd, Garden City Press,
Letchworth, Hertfordshire SG6 1JS.

ISBN: 0 946020 12 4

In the same series:

The Diver Guide to South Devon by K. McDonald and D. Cockbill

The Diver Guide to South Cornwall by Richard Larn

Dive Dorset by John & Vicki Hinchcliffe

The Diver Guide to West Scotland by Gordon Ridley

The Diver Guide to North-West Scotland by Gordon Ridley

Dive Sussex by Kendall McDonald

Great British Wrecks (Vol 1) by Kendall McDonald

Great British Wrecks (Vol 2) by Kendall McDonald

Contents

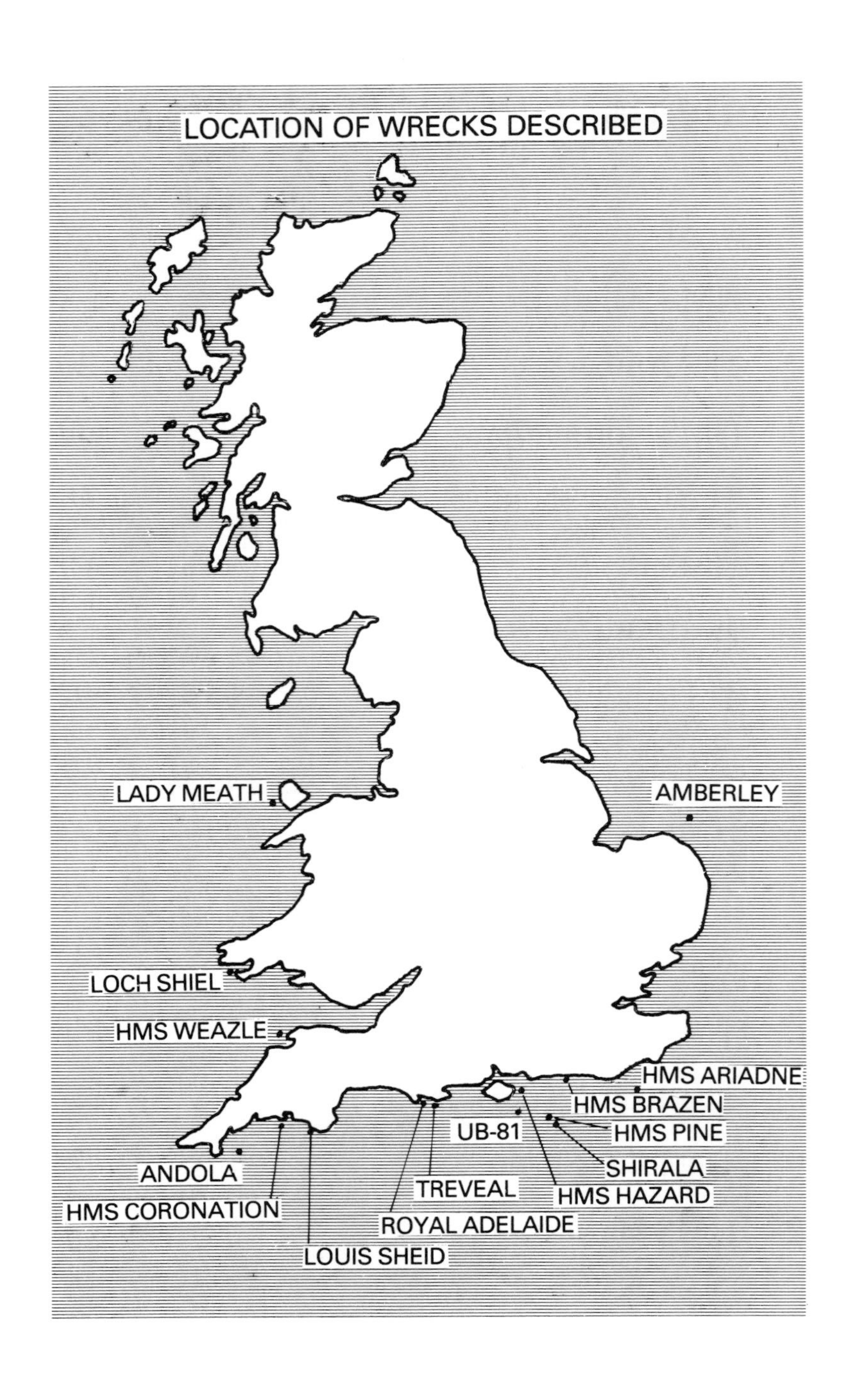
LOCATION OF WRECKS DESCRIBED
LADY MEATH
AMBERLEY
LOCH SHIEL
HMS WEAZLE
HMS ARIADNE
HMS BRAZEN
UB-81
HMS PINE
SHIRALA
ANDOLA
TREVEAL
HMS HAZARD
HMS CORONATION
ROYAL ADELAIDE
LOUIS SHEID

Foreword

MORE SHIPS HAVE SUNK around the coasts of Britain than any other country in the world. In fact, it is impossible to stand on any part of our coast facing the sea and not be looking out over the graves of at least a dozen ships. And each will have had a different reason for her sinking.

Here in Volume Three of the Great British Wrecks series are the stories of another 15 of those shipwrecks – stories which can only add enormously to the thrill of diving these lost ships.

Here are the stories of warships, both old and new, of sailing ships and steamers, of daring rescues and terrible losses. Here for the serious wreck-diver are the facts about those triumphs and tragedies which bring a new understanding of the remains he or she can explore on the seabed.

KENDALL McDONALD

CHAPTER ONE

HMS Ariadne

THEY CALLED THEIR periscopes the "asparagus". They nicknamed the mines they sowed at the entrances to British ports "pineapples". For depth charges, they borrowed a word from the Americans and accepted that they were "ash cans". But despite this schoolboyish humour, it would be a mistake to think them anything else but professionals, who carried with them on each mission an up-to-date copy of *Lloyds Register of Shipping*, all the better to identify their "kills". These were the submarine commanders of the German Navy in World War One. They were young, but those who served in high-risk operations like those undertaken by the Flanders Flotilla were clearly seen to be prematurely aged by stress, particularly by the knowledge that they were unlikely to live for very long. The average life of any U-boat in the Flanders Flotilla was six trips. And at one time the Flanders base was losing one boat a week.

Some U-boat commanders were chivalrous. Some, despite their noble origins, were the dregs. "Brutes they were when they began the war," said Arthur Balfour, the British Foreign Secretary, when hearing of a U-boat atrocity, "and, as far as I can judge, brutes they remain!" But no one could argue that they were not brave. They went out time and time again, knowing that on each trip the odds were shortening against them, as the Allied attempts to bottle them up in their Bruges base grew more and more deadly.

The Flanders Flotilla was rightly described as a thorn in the flesh of the British. From Bruges, the U-boats slipped out into the Channel from either Ostend or Zeebrugge after coming down the canals from their concrete pens. These U-boats were divided into "attack" boats, the UB classes, or the UC type which were minelayers. Their size was considered small – 5-600 tons, with a length of about 180 feet, carrying 23 to 31 crewmen and two or three officers. However, their size bore no relation to the number of their kills, which were so numerous that at one time Britain and the Allies could not produce enough ships to keep up with the losses. And it is no exaggeration to say that at one time at the height of the 1917 sinkings, Britain was nearly faced with the choice of surrendering or starving. Nearly, but not quite, for slowly the Allies learned how to tame the U-boat menace which at one time was sinking 130 merchantmen a month in home waters.

The key to the whole campaign against the U-boat was first to block up the Flanders Flotilla in their bases, and secondly to make life hell – and short – for any that did try to roam down the Channel, seeking Allied shipping. The ways of making the U-boat crews feel that the game was not worth the candle were many and varied. There was the Dover Barrage, with three lines of sudden death. First came the nets, festooned with mines, set just below the water. Behind that were patrol boats waiting to catch any U-boat commander sneaking through on the surface. After this first line came a second barrier of mines anchored in tiers at all depths, designed to make the submarines risk a surface crossing, where more patrol boats were waiting. At night things were not much better for the outward or inward bound U-boat. The Dover Straits were lit from shore to shore by burning magnesium floating on the water, and the U-boat could find itself faced with a belt of flickering flame. But the burning magnesium sometimes went out, and so dark gaps could be found. The U-boat commanders learned to wait for the flame to gutter out and then race through on the surface. It was a gamble, for sometimes the magnesium would flare up again where once it appeared to have been completely extinguished. Barrier three was a more reliable light. Giant searchlights were mounted on both the French and English sides of the Straits at the narrowest part, and their beams met in mid-Channel. Scores of patrol boats hung around the edges of the light, and drifters hung their steel nets out to catch not fish but subs.

This wasn't all. To bottle up the submarines closer to home line of mine-studded nets was laid directly in front of the Fland Flotilla base. Eighteen miles out from Zeebrugge the nets ra miles from the shallow water outside Dunkirk to the sandba the Sheldt. There was not enough water to get under the ne could the U-boats get around the ends. So once again the UC boats had to slide over at night and chance getting c one of the Royal Navy patrols. All this, of course, pla submariners' nerves. But their discipline was never br even after one February day in 1918 when 18 Zeebrugge to run the blockade. And only two came

of insanity as a result of the nervous tension, the cramped conditions, the losses of friends, and the stories of crews who themselves had escaped death by a hair's breadth, did occur. But they were surprisingly rare. Not that the U-boat crews were unaware of the risks. Nor were they stupid. All of them were, until the last months of the war, volunteers. And the increased risks they ran were recognised with better food in their messes, longer leave, and other privileges, including special rewards for sinkings. Even so, in the later stages of the war some members of submarine crews were noted to have a kind of shell shock. Veterans who had hundreds of hours of underwater time suddenly lost all will-power and sense of responsibility. Mind you, by the end of 1917 there were not many veterans left!

The Royal Navy crews who hunted the undersea killers began to note signs of this "shell shock" – foolish mistakes on the part of the submariners and other erratic behaviour that they rightly put down to the numbers of inexperienced men among the crews who had been hurriedly trained to make up the U-boat losses. And there were some men whom the Royal Navy would dearly have liked to make a foolish mistake. These were the leading U-boat commanders whose names were well-known to their hunters – German commanders rarely made any secret of their own names when cross-questioning some hapless merchantman's crew as the U-boat which had sunk them surfaced alongside the lifeboats. So the Navy knew about the submarine "aces" of the Flanders Flotilla – Johann Lohs of *UB-57*, Salzwedel of *UC-71*, Howaldt of *UB-40*, Ramien of *UB-109*, and Pustkuchen of *UC-66* to name only a few of the high-scorers. But there was one man more than any other whom the Navy would like to have depth-charged out of existence – Kapitanleutnant Otto Steinbrinck, the ace of all the Flanders captains, who sank 210,000 tons of Allied shipping, and commanded first *UB-10*, then *UB-18*, *UB-57*, and finally *UC-65*. He completed 24 missions, more than any other German submarine commander in the whole of the war, and was fourth in the scoring table of total tonnages sunk by submarine commanders of the German Navy.

A dark, slender, quiet man, Otto Steinbrinck was a cool customer, and rightly highly popular with his crew. He was held in high regard by the British Navy too for his courage and professionalism, even though any one of the captains who hunted him would have been proud to have been the man who finished his career. Steinbrinck's courage was not of the dashing devil-may-care type, but more one which came from a studied calculation of the risk. His professionalism was the result of serious application to his work. One particular British submarine commander who crossed swords with Steinbrinck was, later, full of admiration for him. He described the incident like this:

"It happened in 1916 on the North Sea coast near Yarmouth. Steinbrinck was in one of the early small German boats and was submerged to 25 feet when looking through his periscope he saw four British submarines running on the surface. They were heading North towards him at a rate of about 12 knots. They were strung out about a mile apart. I know all this because I was the commander of one of those British E-class boats. Steinbrinck attacked the leader of the oncoming craft, which was commanded by a friend of mine. This British officer saw the German's periscope, put his helm hard over, eluded the torpedo, and rammed. Steinbrinck lowered his periscope in time, but got his bow net-cutter – the big saw-edged blade a submarine uses to cuts its way out of nets – caught and bent down. He dived under the British sub and took a periscope peep from the other side. The British boat which was *E-22*, turned back at full speed for another ram when Steinbrinck flicked out both bow torpedoes for a fluke shot. One torpedo hit. It blew up the British boat, which sank at once, leaving two men swimming.

"Steinbrinck saw the other three submarines coming at him swiftly. He then saw them all submerge at once, almost as though at a single command. Their periscopes cut through the water towards the scene of the explosion. They were approaching at short range, and Steinbrinck knew they would let their torpedoes go the moment they got their sights on him. I remember that down in my conning tower I was waiting eagerly with all four torpedoes ready to go as I came along, twenty-five feet down and nine knots speed. Steinbrinck then came to the surface. I met him after the war and compared notes with him. He told me he was damned nervous as he brought his boat up out of the water. He expected to be blown up at any moment. He kept his stern to our line of fire so as to present the smallest possible mark for us to shoot at. He steered his boat over to the spot where *E-22* had sunk. We wondered what he was up to. A couple of German sailors hopped out on deck and leaned down to the water. They were picking up the two Englishmen who has been left swimming when their boat had sunk. Then having rescued the two men, the gallant Steinbrinck dived as fast as he could and got away from there. Well, I wouldn't have done it. I take reasonable risks, but well I'd like to tell a girl I had done it!"

No wonder the British Navy had time for Otto Steinbrinck. But that didn't make them any less keen to catch him. Another exploit on July 26, 1917, made them even keener. Steinbrinck was a great believer in running the Dover Barrage submerged. Many of his colleagues used to dash over the top of the mined nets, but not Steinbrinck. He went as deep as he could and eased his boat through. And July 26, 1917, was no different. In fact on that day Steinbrinck started his submerged run almost as soon as he left Zeebrugge in *UC-65* and set a record, completing the longest-ever submerged run through the straits in the early hours of that day. He was considerably surprised when he surfaced to find a damned great British cruiser filling up his periscope eyepiece. Minutes later he had correctly identified the monster as HMS *Ariadne*.

HMS *Ariadne* was built in 1898 and, at the time she was planned, it was thought that there would be a place in the sea warfare then developing for a fast, heavily-armed commerce raider. So she was built at John Brown's with 18,000 horse power engines and huge Belleville boilers which were intended to make her one of the fastest cruisers afloat. Unfortunately, the weight of the armour plate fitted to this 11,000-ton ship slowed her down a lot. Speed trials shortly after her commissioning at Portsmouth in June, 1902, showed that she could only manage 20.75 knots flat out. Even so she became the flagship for Admiral Sir A. L. Douglas while he was Commander-in-Chief of the North American and West Indies station. After those moments of glory, by 1908 she had been relegated to be tender to the *Barfleur*, and just before the outbreak of the 1914-1918 war she was further demoted to the training service. She was, in fact, obsolete almost as soon as she was launched.

In July, 1917, the *Ariadne* was allowed to adopt a belligerent role – but only to lay mines in the Northern Barrage, which entailed setting a wall of mines across the 240 miles from the Orkneys to Norway, so bottling up the German U-boats and German shipping and stopping their exit into the Atlantic. So on July 26, 1917, HMS *Ariadne*, laden with mines, lumbered up the Channel towards the Royal Sovereign light vessel. If she had been crewed as planned she would have had 677 officers and men packed into her 462-foot-long hull. But as she was only to operate as a mine-layer, there was just a nucleus crew aboard. They manned most of her 16 six-inch guns and dozen 12-pounders. Her two torpedo tubes were unmanned, just as they had been for most of her service, and there were no torpedoes aboard. But there were some close by, and in *UC-65* fingers itched to give them to the *Ariadne*. Steinbrinck could hardly believe that this big cruiser was not surrounded by heavily-armed escorts, but periscope sweeps of the whole horizon told him that *Ariadne* was only supported by two small destroyers and some launches. For such a big prize they were a risk he was prepared to take.

It was clear too, that Captain Harry Hesketh-Smyth, D.S.O., R.N., on *Ariadne's* bridge was totally unaware of the presence of *UC-65*. He too was a war veteran, having been mentioned in despatches for his bravery in an action on October 25, 1916. This decoration was followed by the award of the DSO in February, 1917. It was a storm-clouded morning in the Channel. The depressions were pushing over from France – in fact an air battle over the British front line was broken up by a thunderstorm of such violence that four of our aircraft were missing. Otto Steinbrinck fired only one torpedo at the big cruiser. It went home amidships on her port side – and the resulting explosion was enormous. All the mines on board HMS *Ariadne* went off at once.

Thirty-eight men were killed instantly. Nine more were badly wounded. She sank down in 19m of water and stayed upright long enough for her escorts to take off all the other crew members. Not long after the last man, Captain Harry Hesketh-Smyth, left the ship, she rolled over and sank down on her starboard side. The escorts criss-crossed the area angrily, dropping depth charges on any likely echo. But Otto Steinbrinck and *UC-65* were not one of them, and he slid safely away from yet another of his many kills.

Otto Steinbrinck survived the war. He became a highly successful businessman in Berlin, and was often to be seen lunching at the Kaiserhof. Some of his guests were the former Royal Navy captains who had tried so hard to kill him during the war! But his last boat, *UC-65*, did not survive. It was lost when being commanded by Kapitanleutnant Klaus Lafrenz on November 3, 1917. Confronted by a British submarine when he was on the surface about to enter Zeebrugge returning from a long mission, Kapitan Lafrenz made one of those silly mistakes that too many missions and too much strain brought out in the men of the Flanders Flotilla. He told his No. 2, as he saw the British sub turning to aim its bow tubes at him, that it was perfectly simple to dodge torpedoes – you merely waited for the compressed air surface "boil" of the torpedo discharge and immediately put the helm hard over. As he spoke he saw the air boil from the British sub and swerved sharply. Unfortunately for Lafrenz the British sub, *C-15*, had fired a double bow shot and though he avoided one the other took *UC-65* full square and amidships. Captain Lafrenz and his Leutnant were among the five survivors out of a crew of 28 who were picked up by *C-15*.

Diving the Ariadne

THE *ARIADNE* IS AT 50 42 52; 00 23 29 E. She is well out in the Channel near the Royal Sovereign Light, and so must be a hard-boat dive. Such boats can be hired from Newhaven or Rye. Eastbourne Sub-Aqua Club (BS-AC No. 513) warn, however, that anyone diving this distance out must keep a constant watch for coastal shipping "clipping" the coast around Beachy Head. They say that such ships pass both sides of the Light Tower with scant regard for dive boats displaying the "A" Flag.

The cruiser was badly broken by the explosion of the mines aboard, and was further broken up between 1923 and 1925 by the explosive charges used by the Ocean Salvage and Towing Company to disperse her under contract to Trinity House. By September 14, 1925, they were able to report that nothing stood more than "45 feet above the seabed" Salvage went on over the years. By 1981 sea and salvage had dispersed her over a huge area, and there is nothing left standing higher than four metres above the seabed.

Salvage work started up again in 1984, and the ship is now broken into two sections, even if it is difficult to know exactly where one section ends and the other begins. But the bow section does point towards the Royal Sovereign. Salvage work was done at one time by grabs, and as a result mines which did not explode at the time of the torpedo attack are now broken open and guncotton is exposed. These mines are scattered around the area, with some reported by divers on the Long Shoal, jammed into gullies in the rocks. There are more on the Horse of Willingdon, a rocky outcrop nearly a mile in length near the Royal Sovereign

Shoals, so divers on and around the *Ariadne* should take great care.

And divers wanting a rummage should remember that much of the wreckage has extremely sharp edges. One diver whose SMB line was cut on such a piece is said to have been picked up seven miles away! It is, it is true, an area of strong currents. A deal of the wreckage is buried under the sand, and there is a story, told by divers, that an entire engine room was missed by the salvors and lies buried, intact, to this day! General depth in the area is 19 metres.

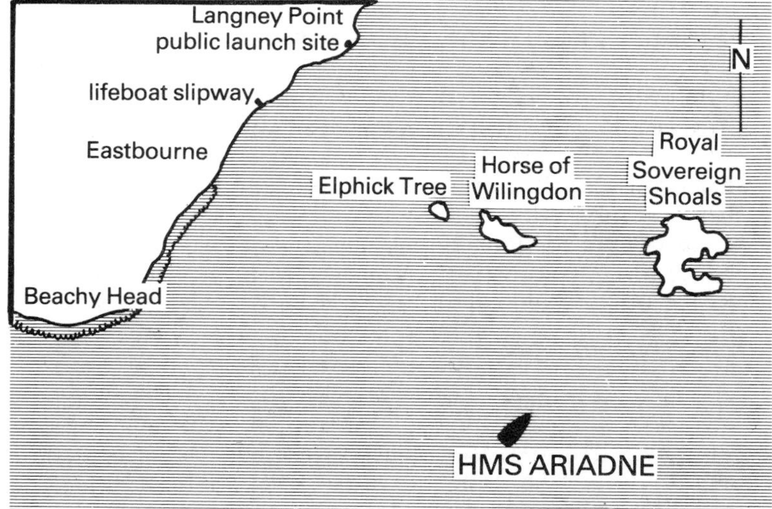

The 'Ariadne' is well out in the Channel, widely dispersed in about 19 metres of water.

Ariadne wreck log

Position: 50 42 52; 00 23 29E.

Off Royal Sovereign Light, Sussex

Chart No.: 536

Date: ....

Dive leader: ....

Equipment used:
ABLJ/STAB .... Air capacity: ....

Suit.. Demand valve ....

Weights: .... SMB/reel ....

Special equipment ....

Dive Boat:..

Weather..........................Sea Height...........State of tide...........

Current ....Underwater viz ....

Dive timing:
Left surface ....Returned surface...........................

Maximum depth:...

Decompression required...

Seabed type.............................Scour present ....

State of wreckage ....

Area of ship dived: ....

Special points to note: ....

....

CHAPTER TWO

The Amberley

BLACK AS THE 2290 tons of coal in her belly were the clouds which threatened the *Amberley* – and the wind was still rising. The 2405-ton collier rolled violently as huge seas slapped her about. Spray lashed across her bridge windows, and when that cleared there were rattling sheets of hail to blind her. It was April 2, 1973. Gale warnings were in operation all along the East Coast, but Captain John Black of the *Amberley* already knew that this was a big one. It was clear to this experienced seaman that the wind was still rising, and the state of the sea was more akin to a Force 10 than any ordinary common-or-garden gale. The waves with crests overhanging their dark green walls, seemed poised to smash him. In moments of clear visibility, great patches of foam formed, only to be torn away in long white streaks. The voyage of the *Amberley*, which had seemed at first to be just another trip and just another load of coal to be carried from Goole, on the Humber, to Shoreham, Sussex, was turning very nasty indeed.

Captain Black, though he could hear nothing but the howl of the wind, felt that something was wrong beneath his feet. The *Amberley* seemed to be leaning more and more to starboard, and never quite seemed to come upright, or not for very long. He tried to put out of his mind what he guessed was happening, but finally there could be no doubt – his cargo of coal was shifting. *Amberley* had taken on a list which in those seas of over 30 feet high meant disaster. Cromer Coastguard picked up his radio call.

On the tarmac at Coltishall RAF Station in Norfolk the big Whirlwind helicopters shuddered in the violent gusts of wind, and some aircrew in 22 Squadron Search and Rescue began to have doubts about getting airborne at all that day. Certainly if the wind increased any more all flying must be cancelled. Further North at Leconfield, in Yorkshire, the same thoughts were running through the minds of the men of 202 Squadron. The wind was being measured in gusts of 65 knots. The helicopter crews were not the only people on full alert. Cromer Coastguard had now

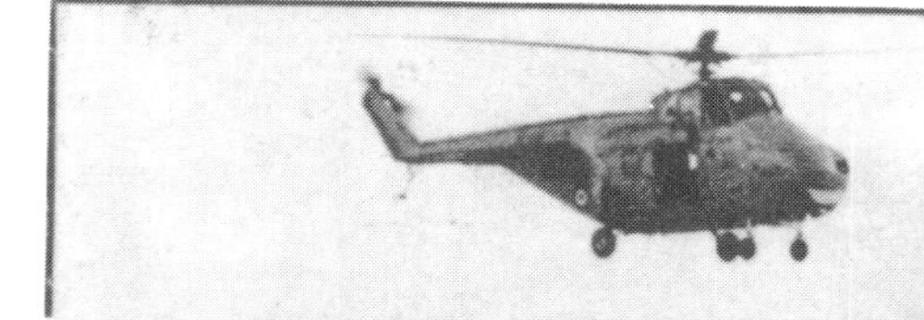

●WHILE firemen of the Norfolk Brigade stand by, an SAR Whirlwind of 202 Squadron comes in to land on the sports field at Wells-next-the-Sea, bringing to safety the first six crew members rescued from a gale-damaged ship.

'Copter crews in North Sea rescue drama

THE SECOND of April will always be a day to remember for 22 Squadron. For it was on that day that they took over from 202 Squadron and it was halfway through the handover ceremony at Coltishall that they got an emergency rescue call-out.

It was precisely 16.15 — just as Sqn Ldr John Hoskin was in the middle of taking over from Sqn Ldr Bob Reekie of 202 Squadron — that the distress call came through from the 1,950-ton collier Amberley, drifting helplessly in a hurricane-force gale in the North Sea.

Immediately two Whirlwinds, crewed by Flt Lts Jim Ross, [illegible] Cass (navigator), M Sig Ken Meagher; Flt Lts Ian Christie-Miller, Don Arnold (navigator) and Sgt Dick Amor, took off to rescue the ship's 16-man crew.

With them — but just slightly ahead of them — was a Whirlwind from B Flight of 202 Squadron from Leconfield crewed by Flt Lt Bob Braithwaite, M Nav Ron Dedmen and M AEOp "Dinty" More.

The Leconfield crew got to the helpless ship first and, after dumping fuel, managed to lift off six of the crew. But they very nearly did not make it. For on the outward journey they faced headwinds up to 70 mph and snowstorms.

The Coltishall crews, too, had a rough trip. It took them 25 minutes to cover the 15 miles to the coast. And when they got over the sinking ship and M Sig Ken Meagher reached the deck to lift off some of the crew, he came close to disaster when the ship took an extra steep lurch and almost pitched him into the sea.

For the crew of an 8 Squadron Shackleton, diverted to help out, the situation appeared extremely dangerous for they signalled an "Expedite" order as it appeared to them that the ship was likely to go down at any moment.

At one time the ship's instruments indicated a list of more than 55 degrees — in fact the pointer of the inclinometer was as far [illegible] as it would go.

Since the rescue both squadrons have received grateful letters thanking them for rescuing the skipper, Mr. John Black of Newcastle and his crew, from near-certain death.

Newspaper report shows helicopter landing with survivors of the 'Amberley' wreck.

linked with the Northern Rescue Co-ordination Centre. Ambulances were on stand-by. Police opened up rescue procedures. And some 70 men became directly concerned with the *Amberley's* safety.

The *Amberley* was now listing some 20 degrees to starboard, taking in water. Captain Black knew it was only a matter of time unless he could keep her head-on to the mammoth seas. And then his steering went. Cromer passed the message. The Whirlwind helicopter at Coltishall was scrambled. The *Amberley* was now

Crew members run from the RAF rescue helicopter that saved them.

drifting helplessly towards the Dudgeon Shoal off the Norfolk coast, but battling towards her was the first Whirlwind helicopter of 22 Squadron. Aboard was Master Signaller Kenneth Meagher – the duty winchman. He could see the sea below them and didn't like what he saw. It was late afternoon now, and the black skies threatened an early end to the light. In the helicopter they heard Captain Black's next message. It said everything in one short transmission: "Situation now critical. Make all speed. Unable to launch life-boats ..." Soon the *Amberley* was underneath the Whirlwind. The first pass made the Captain's message seem an understatement. The 262-foot-long *Amberley* was beam-on to 30-foot high waves and listing so heavily to starboard that it seemed a wonder she was afloat at all. What happened next is best told in the words of the *London Gazette* of October 30 that same year, in the citation of an Air Force Cross to Master Signaller Meagher:

"With complete disregard to his personal safety, Master Signaller Meagher allowed himself to be lowered to the *Amberley*.

During his approach to the stricken vessel he was buffeted by 65-knot gusts of wind and subjected to flying spray and occasional hail. Nevertheless, he succeeded by great agility and determination in boarding the restricted area of the bridge which was rolling violently and so heavily that it afforded a precarious footing. Regardless of the danger to his own life, Master Signaller Meagher detached himself from the aircraft and prepared to send the survivors singly to the helicopter. Two seamen were rescued by this method. While the second survivor was being winched to the helicopter the ship rolled even more violently and the stanchion which Master Signaller Meagher was using as a hand-hold broke. He was thrown heavily against the wheelhouse, badly bruising his leg, but he continued to direct the winch operator. At this stage the Master and Radio Operator refused to leave the ship, and so Master Signaller Meagher rescued the third survivor by double lift, accompanying him to the helicopter. Disregarding his injury, and fully aware of the dangers involved, Master Signaller Meagher was lowered twice more to rescue a further two sailors from the stern area of the *Amberley*, where the pitching movement made his task very difficult. By his quiet, dogged determination, great courage and exceptional devotion to duty, Master Signaller Meagher was responsible for saving the lives of five seamen at great risk to his own safety."

There were now 11 men left on *Amberley*, but more help was on the way. Another Whirlwind from Coltishall had been scrambled, and so had one from Leconfield. One by one the crew were lifted off by the helicopters. Now only the Captain and the Radio Operator remained. Sergeant Richard James Amor, of Coltishall, who was to win the Air Force Medal for his actions, had already been hauled up three times with survivors in the rescue strop from the slippery, canted stern of the sinking ship, but he went down twice more to take off the radio man and finally Captain Black. He was only just in time. As Captain Black was pulled up to the safety of the helicopter, the seas closed over his ship. By using the classic understatement that we expect from those involved in such rescues, one of the helicopter squadron crews revealed the real conditions that ruled that afternoon: "It was a particularly hazardous rescue operation. We got there in the nick of time ..." In fact, if conditions had been only slightly worse the helicopter rescue would have been out of the question. Two more Air Force Crosses were awarded to the men from Leconfield, and there were also three Queen's Commendations.

Overleaf: war artist Rex Flood's painting of the rescue.

Sgt Dick Amor (centre) won the Air Force Medal, and Flt Lt. Tony Cass (left) and Flt. Lt. Don Arnold (right) received the Queen's commendation after the 'Amberley' rescue.

All of which makes the sinking of the *Amberley* and the rescue of her whole crew a classic in the heroic records of the RAF's helicopter squadrons.

Diving the Amberley

THE *AMBERLEY* IS AT 53 02 55; 00 58 12 E. A steel ship of 262 feet long with a beam of 38 feet, she was built in 1953 by Grangemouth Dockyard Company, and has an eight-cylinder oil engine built by British Polar Engines of Glasgow. She lies in 20 metres of water on a sand seabed from which she is 10 metres proud, and virtually intact. She is leaning over on her port side with a deep scour on that side.

The *Amberley* was the first ship to be bought by the British Sub-Aqua Club for the benefit of all divers, so no souvenirs please! Her position is four-and-a-half miles due North of Blakeney Harbour, which dries. Best launch place is at Cley Next the Sea, further to the East, or at Weybourne. Inflatable and small boat cox'ns must remember that it is a long run out to the wreck, and plenty of spare fuel must be carried. On a calm day there is turbulence over the wreck, which is sometimes buoyed. She lies on the outer edge of the Blakeney overfalls, and is just out from the drop-off, so close in fact that her bow nudges the bank. A course of 167 Magnetic on Blakeney Tower should put a boat into the area of the wreck when a bearing of between 076 and 088 Magnetic to the Blakeney Overfalls Buoy (dependent on tide and wind) will narrow the search down even further. Viz can reach 30 feet.

THE AMBERLEY

The 'Amberley' lies on sand in 20 metres of water.

A dive boat which often visits the wreck in season is *Elizabeth*, a 31-footer with all electronic gear based in Blakeney Harbour, skippered by Robin Bishop (Tel: Cley (0263) 740200). The *Elizabeth* will take 12 divers, though ten will be more comfortable. As Blakeney is tidal, though the actual trip out to the *Amberley* is only a matter of minutes, the return to berth can take some time, and this delay should be built into the dive planning. Slack on the wreck is about three hours after High.

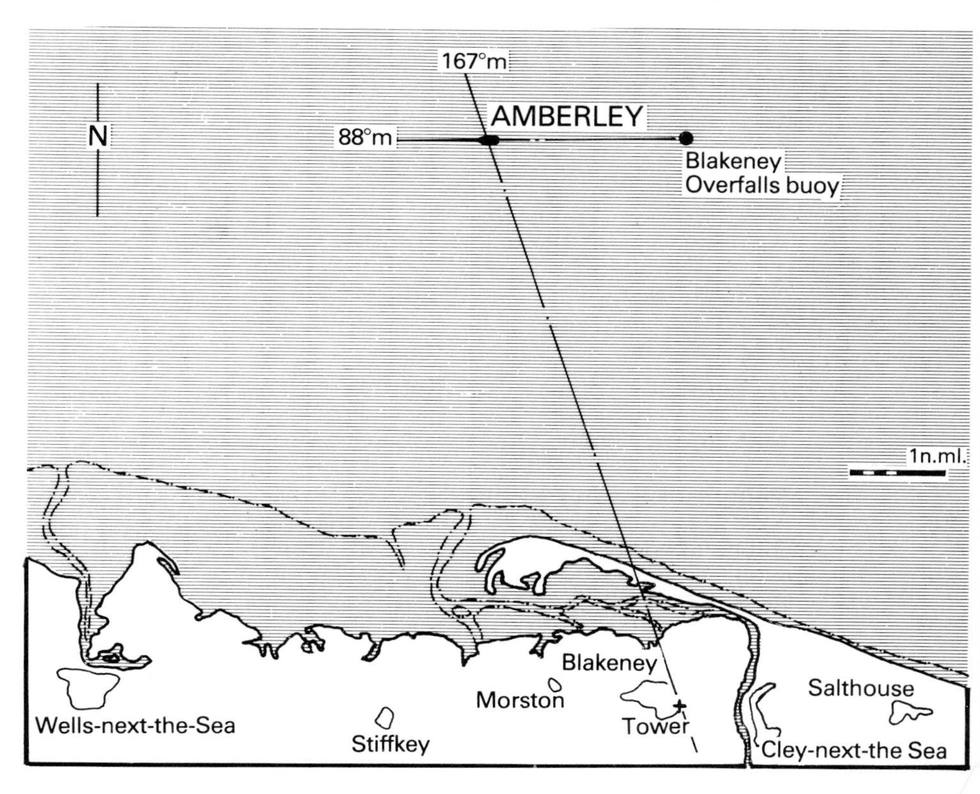

Amberley wreck log

Position: 53 02 55; 00 58 12E.

Blakeney, Norfolk

Chart No.: 108

Date: ....

Dive leader: ....

Equipment used:
ABLJ/STAB .... Air capacity: ....

Suit .... Demand valve ....

Weights: .... SMB/reel ....

Special equipment ....

Dive Boat: ....

Weather .... Sea Height .... State of tide ....

Current .... Underwater viz ....

Dive timing:
Left surface .... Returned surface ....

Maximum depth: ....

Decompression required ....

Seabed type .... Scour present ....

State of wreckage ....

Area of ship dived: ....

Special points to note: ....

....

....

....

....

....

....

....

....

....

....

CHAPTER THREE

HMS Coronation

ON THE SEABED cannon point out from the rocks which act as gun-carriages. Nearby lies the ball ammunition for them, so sea-swollen now that it will never slide down any muzzle. Anyone who dives Penlee Point, which is only just in Cornish territory on the Western side of Plymouth Sound, can be in no doubt that here lies the evidence of a great shipwreck. And so it is. For this is the final graveyard of Captain Charles Skelton and 600 men of the Royal Navy who died when their ship, the 1427-ton 90-gun *Coronation* capsized on September 3, 1691. If anyone could have saved his ship it should have been Skelton. He had the luck a sea captain needs, and the experience to go with it, for his rise to fame and fortune had started long before his shipwreck, way back in 1672, when he was appointed to be Second Lieutenant of His Majesty's Ship *Gloucester*.

To a large extent the future of any young officer was made by the ship to which he was appointed. If the ship took good prizes, he would, by his rank, be entitled to a good share of the booty. And that again depended on the skill and daring of the ship's captain. Skelton was lucky in his captain – for John Holmes was not lacking in daring. And despite the fact that in 1672 Holmes was only just in his thirties, he had seen more than his share of sea battles, and had been promoted on results time and time again. John Holmes was a man much talked of as destined for high office – and not just because his brother was Admiral Sir Robert Holmes. It was therefore no wonder that in 1672 young Charles Skelton was delighted to be serving under John Holmes. His satisfaction was complete when he found that the *Gloucester* was one of a squadron commanded by his own captain's brother, the famous Sir Robert. Only one thing may have marred his total happiness. To take prizes it is almost necessary to have a war on your hands. And at the moment – January 1672 – there was no war. True, there was a feeling in the air. And Samuel Pepys, the determined Clerk of the Acts of the Navy, was appealing desperately for money for

Opposite: a warship of the 'Coronation' class.

the Navy, but that in itself could hardly be taken as a sign of a coming war, for Pepys seemed to do little else.

But there were people who knew for sure that a war was coming. England must have a great fleet by the spring, for the King and his Ministers were now committed to a secret alliance with the French. Their aim was to destroy the Dutch Republic. England was to sink her fleet and seize her colonies. The French army would attack her on land. In February the hustle started. The first, second and third-rate ships were made ready. But years of neglect did not make the preparation of a great fleet all that easy. Though Charles Skelton joined his ship at Portsmouth, the *Gloucester* was, like other men-of-war, scarcely ready for sea. And by no means all the ships were even there, let alone prepared for action. Sir Robert Holmes flew his flag in the *St Michael*, and of them all she was probably the best prepared. From the deck of the *Gloucester* Skelton could see other great ships. Close at hand was the *Resolution*, commanded by Thomas Butler, Earl of Ossory. There too was the *Cambridge* of Captain Hollis, Captain Legg's *Fairfax* and the *York*, commanded by Captain Elliott. The lighters went back and forth between the men-of-war, loading shot and powder, provisions and stores of all kinds.

Though there could be little doubt that action was planned very soon, Skelton knew that his captain, John Holmes, was far from satisfied with the stores that the *Gloucester* had so far managed to get on board. And all the time as the stores came aboard the rumours came with them. Skelton had a vast admiration for his captain, and this esteem never faltered, despite the endless drills that Holmes put his crews through during this waiting time. Daring Holmes was, but daring without a well-trained and disciplined ship's company was not enough. Between drills young John Holmes – and Skelton with him – fumed over the slowness with which his ship was being made ready for war.

On board the *St Michael*, Sir Robert fumed even more. He must have known of the King's design, and that war would be soon forced upon the Dutch. In the first few days of March he could stand the waiting no longer. He sent a rider with a letter from Portsmouth to London, requesting permission to attack home-coming Dutch ships in the Channel. And by a relay of horses his reply came galloping back. It was the answer he wanted. Despite the fact that no declaration of war had been made, he was given permission to attack any Dutch ships he found. The reason for Sir Robert's impatience to get to grips with the Dutch may well have been patriotism. It may, on the other hand, also have had something to do with the fact that the Dutch Smyrna Fleet was on its way up-Channel, laden with silks and precious good from the East.

A hurried conference with his captains followed his receipt of permission to attack Dutch shipping. Sir Robert was going to sail regardless of how many ships he could take with him – his whole fleet should have numbered 36 men-of-war. He had in fact five, including the *St Michael*. And with those he sailed to meet nearly 60 Dutch merchant ships, guarded by a dozen men-of-war. True, surprise was on his side, but even such a dirty trick was hardly likely to weigh much in his favour when the shooting started. Young John Holmes was furious when he found that he and the *Gloucester*, plus two other ships, would be delayed several hours behind his brother's little squadron. The reason for this we do not know. It may have been a shortage of stores; it was certainly not planned – for Sir Robert could do with every ship available.

On March 12, 1672, Sir Robert made contact with the Dutch Smyrna Fleet off the Isle of Wight. The Dutch were, it seems, not expecting trouble, and so were surprised by Sir Robert's demand to their Admiral that he should strike his colours. It was about noon when the meeting took place. With the *St Michael* were *Resolution*, *Cambridge*, *Fairfax* and *York*. Lest we think too hardly of Sir Robert, it is only fair to say that an eye-witness (from the *Resolution*) of this encounter does say in the State Papers of Charles II that Sir Robert fired a warning gun, announced his identity, and called upon the Dutch Admiral to strike. The Dutch Admiral appears to have been puzzled by this request – as well he might, as war had not been declared – and sent his lieutenant aboard *St Michael* to obtain clarification. The Dutch lieutenant did not, apparently, take too kindly to Sir Robert's ultimatum. "Having given some saucy language to Sir Robert", he was promptly clapped into the hold, and the fight started with a burst of small shot and full broadside from the *St Michael*. The Dutch seem to have tumbled very quickly to what was happening, because the eye-witness on *Resolution* notes that they formed a line and put their merchantmen on the other side of it.

Sir Robert was, it seems, caught out by this manœuvre, for the whole Dutch line passed him, pouring in shot after shot. By six o'clock that night Sir Robert's *St Michael* was pretty badly shot up, and, in fact, he found the ship so disabled that he moved his flag from the *St Michael* to the *Cambridge*. The fight was now moving down Channel, and Charles Skelton in *Gloucester* could hear the sound of guns from far away. The truth was that the Dutch were putting up such a stout defence that Sir Robert's impetuosity looked very likely to bring about an English defeat. He obviously had not reckoned on the eleven men-of-war, which carried from 40 to 50 guns each, nor on the fact that the 56 merchantmen were not all sitting ducks. (In fact, some 16 to 20 of them carried between 20 and 30 guns apiece.) As a result of their fire, the *St Michael* was badly disabled, and the *Resolution* did not look in much better shape. The balance of power when the next day would dawn looked very much in favour of the Dutch.

This balance was tipped slightly by the arrival at the scene of battle very early in the morning of young John Holmes and his *Gloucester*, together with the *Sussex* and another ship. It was hardly a pleasant first glimpse of the face of war for young Charles Skelton. Before this he had only seen the *St Michael* trim and smart and decorative. Now he saw a shambles; her rigging in tatters, all her decks shattered, the marks of fire and the holes of shot everywhere. But worst of all, laid out on the foredeck were rows of wounded, moaning and twisting with pain. And there were other silent rows, faces covered with whatever came to hand, as though to protect them against the coming dawn.

At first light the battle was joined again. By now the fight had drifted down to Rye, and soon it seemed the Dutch would be back in their home waters with very little loss, despite the English treachery. Skelton had little time to ponder on the fruits of war, for in the first light Captain John Holmes ordered all hands to action stations. The sails filled with the morning breeze and the 50-gun *Gloucester* bore straight down on the 54-gun *Hollandia*, the flagship of the Dutch Rear-Admiral Van Nes. Closer and closer went the *Gloucester*, and Skelton's nerves must have been strained to breaking-point – for despite the storm of small shot and ball that the *Hollandia* and her sister ships poured upon them, John Holmes held his fire. Closer and closer, and now the *Hollandia's* sides loomed above the *Gloucester*, but still there came no order to fire. Finally, with a crunch of wood on wood, the *Gloucester* and *Hollandia* were locked "arme and arme". At that moment came the order to the *Gloucester's* gunners to fire. The broadside that they fired could not miss. Now the order was to fire at will, and Skelton was far too busy organizing his boarding parties with the *Gloucester's* lieutenant to do more than register each broadside as a rippling shock through the timbers under his feet.

The *Hollandia* was no easily-taken prize. For some hours the battle raged back and forth, but finally Van Nes's crew were forced to strike their colours and their ship was taken into the ranks of the little English fleet. Charles Skelton had borne his fair share of the fighting. In fact he and the first lieutenant had done more than that. Captain Holmes had, at the height of the action, staggered back with a lead ball from some Dutch musket or carronade in his chest. The wound was serious, but not critical, but it did mean that Holmes was out of the later stages of the action. The *Hollandia* had 80 bales of fine silk aboard as well as "much plate". And seeing it, Skelton could almost calculate his share. Looking at the *Hollandia* from the damaged decks of the *Gloucester* it seemed surprising that the Dutch ship still floated. The *Gloucester's* prize crew obviously felt the same surprise, and some time was spent in transferring at least some of the loot to English ships. They were right – after a few hours of occupation, the *Hollandia* gave one warning lurch from side to side and then swiftly sank.

Sir Robert saw her sink from the deck of the *Cambridge*, and knew that *Resolution* and his former flagship the *St Michael* were not in a much better shape. So as soon as night fell he ordered these two damaged ships to the Downs and then continued the chase of the Dutch with what ships he had left. So the running fight continued up the Channel until finally the next night the Dutch drew away as the wind increased and headed for home. Sir Robert came ashore at Sandwich, and brought with him five Dutch merchantmen that he had taken as prizes. *Gloucester's* second lieutenant, Charles Skelton, was now to reap the reward for his coolness in the action against the *Hollandia*. His captain, John Holmes, was knighted for his bravery, and as soon as he was sufficiently recovered from his wound, was given command of the *Rupert*. Sir John noted Skelton's conduct in the Smyrna Fleet action as "highly approved", and when he took command of the *Rupert*, took young Skelton with him as "a person in whose tried courage and conduct I can place the highest confidence".

Skelton was on his way up. And his luck held once again when he found himself serving under Lieutenant Edward Russell in the 64-gun *Rupert*. Here his luck lay in serving with a man who bore such a famous name. Edward Russell was only 19, but he was the son of Edward Russell, younger brother of William Russell, first Duke of Bedford. And as such was a useful young man to know. The opportunity to make friends with such a young man would not be one to miss, and there is some evidence in the continuing career of Skelton that they were certainly not enemies. In fact Russell and Skelton fought side by side in the *Rupert* with Sir John Holmes as their captain in the battle of Sole Bay on May 28 1672, only a few months after Skelton had distinguished himself in the *Gloucester*.

The little-known battle of Sole Bay gave some sort of revenge to the Dutch for the unprovoked attack on their Smyrna Fleet. The English and French fleets, about 100 ships in all, had sailed from Portsmouth into the North Sea, and put into Sole Bay, Southwold, to water and refit. It was there that the Dutch admiral De Ruyter found them, and, attacking from the North East with 70 ships, managed to concentrate all his force on the English Blue squadron under the Earl of Sandwich, whose flagship was blown up. At nightfall the Dutch withdrew. Charles Skelton seems once again to have acquitted himself well, for on February 5th 1673, he was given his first command, the *Speedwell*. Not much of a command, a sixth-rater, but at least it was a ship of his own. From then on he worked his way steadily up until on April 12 1678, he was given his first big command – the *Staveereen*, a ship which had been taken from the Dutch at the battle of Sole Bay.

Command now followed command. Charles Skelton obviously was a good commander, and had powerful friends – Sir Robert Holmes, Sir John Holmes (from 1677 to 1679 Admiral and Commander-in-Chief in the Downs), and Edward Russell, now captain successively of such great ships as the *Newcastle*, the *Swiftsure*, the *Tiger*. A good captain with friends in high places was a winning combination in any navy, and the Royal Navy of those times was no exception. The summer of 1680 brought Skelton the command of the *Young Spragge*, and in 1686 the captaincy of the *Constant Warwick*. On November 26 that same year by order of the Commander of the Fleet, Lord Dartmouth, Skelton was upgraded once again to be captain of the *Lyon*. He was riding high, but although his next appointment meant the command of 660 men and a 90-gun ship, and was yet another glory to add to his distinguished career, it was to end in his death and that of many of those who served with him. This appointment came early in 1690 when Captain Charles Skelton was given command of HMS *Coronation*. The appointment led Skelton quickly into his last sea battle.

In the year that Skelton took command of the *Coronation* the affairs of England were in a sorry state. William III had taken almost all the troops there were in the country to fight in Ireland against King James's army. This seemed to Louis XIV of France, who supported James, too much of an opportunity to miss. So he started preparing a great fleet to threaten London and invade England. This invasion would, he felt sure, foment a Jacobite uprising in support of James. The great French fleet was to be made up of two smaller fleets. One under Tourville was at Brest. The other was to be brought round by Chateaurenault from Toulon. The only thing opposing such an invasion force was the Royal Navy, but it was a navy that had been weakened by neglect.

Admiral Killigrew was sent to Cadiz to intercept the Toulon fleet, but missed it. Sir Cloudesly Shovell was away with six ships escorting some of William's forces to Ireland. The absence of these two commanders and their ships left the English fleet in a weak state, and certainly in no shape to fight the 80 ships of the line and fireships under Tourville. The English fleet under the Earl of Torrington had, together with some Dutch ships, 55 warships and 25 fireships. Despite this inferiority Torrington took his fleet out to meet the French to the West of the Isle of Wight. The French declined to fight, for which small mercy Torrington thanked God.

Meanwhile, Edward Russell had been appointed Treasurer of the Navy in 1689 and Admiral of the Blue squadron in the fleet under Torrington. And in 1690, when Torrington was trying to hold off the French, Edward Russell was playing a rather unsavoury role in politics in London. Because of his political services, he felt he should be in command and not Torrington, and it is said that it was his intrigues that resulted in Torrington being ordered, despite his small force, to fight the French fleet. The order came from Queen Mary and her Council, and Torrington had no choice but to seek battle. *Coronation* was one of the ships on which he now had to rely, and it is some measure of the worth in which Skelton was held that Sir Ralph Delavall, Vice-Admiral of the Blue (or rear squadron) chose Skelton and *Coronation* as the ship which would carry his flag, and from which he would command that squadron. Russell, as Admiral of the Blue, should have been in command of that squadron, but was still in London, watching the course of events.

At 8 am on June 30, 1690, the Battle of Beachy Head began. The Dutch ships were in the lead, and were in action within the hour. They fought well, but were caught between the fire of the main French fleet and other French ships which had managed to double round behind them. Then, as the French were in a crescent moon formation, the Blue squadron were heavily engaged, but Torrington and his squadron in the middle of the line could only fire at long range. *Coronation* was in the thick of it, closing often to just musket-shot distance before opening fire. But the wind enabled to French to keep edging away from really close-quarter action until around 2 pm when it dropped, and the real slugging match began. It went on for an hour, and was such a close-to affair that one captain in the Blue squadron reported that shot was going right through his ship. By 4 pm the action ceased and Skelton in *Coronation* was glad of it. He had been hit time and time again, but had given more than he got. The Battle of Beachy Head had been lost – the London gossips said of it that "The Dutch had the honour, the French the advantage, and the English the shame". Certainly Torrington had lost nine ships and withdrew into the Thames, leaving the French masters of the Channel.

On December 23, 1690, Edward Russell was made Commander-in-Chief of the Fleet, and asked Charles Skelton, who had been highly praised for his part in the Battle of Beachy Head, to remain in command of *Coronation* under him. Skelton, though of course he did not know it, had fought his last sea battle. And so had *Coronation*. During the spring and summer of the following year, Russell tried hard to bring the French fleet to battle. The Fleet, of which *Coronation* was now part, consisted of 57 English ships and 17 Dutch, but the French were not to be drawn. Plans were made to attack the French in their ports, but they came to nothing, and not one of the attacks was made. A bad spring was followed by a worse summer. It was windy and rough, and to these difficulties of the Fleet were added the endless, actionless patrolling of the Channel. The log of the *Royal Oak* shows that the Fleet was anchored in Torbay on August 23, 1691. The Fleet is almost certain to have included the *Coronation*; the *Harwich* and the *Northumberland* were there for sure. On Sunday August 30, the *Royal Oak's* log showed them out on another Channel patrol. Great swirling copperplate writing – to fill up the big space left for the first entry on a page under "Remarkable Observation and Accidents" – says: "All Continuing faire and Pleasant Weather. At 8 of ye Clock this morning the West End of ye Lizard Bore NWBW 6 Leagues".

Attempts to lure the French fleet into action were still going on. At noon on Monday August 31 the log-keeper of the *Royal Oak* noted: "Still continuing faire weather and Easy Gailes. At Noon Ushant SSE 10 Leagues". But on the next day, Tuesday September 1 the *Royal Oak* was only five leagues off Ushant and the weather had changed to "squally weather blowing verry fresh" On the 2nd "still continuing squally freshening weather" with Ushant at eight leagues. The Fleet now turned back for Plymouth in the early hours of the morning. The weather was obviously going from bad to worse, and the log of the *Royal Oak* records "verry Squally Stormy weather" as the great ships of the Channel Fleet raced for Plymouth and shelter. The wind that drove them on their way from Ushant to Plymouth was first of all coming from the South, then it swung to the South-West and rushed them on their way, but finally settled in the South-South-East and freshened even more, until it was blowing a full gale. This was the Fleet's undoing. A friendly wind blowing them home had now turned into a killer. A South-South-East gale was blowing almost at right angles across the entrance to Plymouth Harbour. But one by one they tried to enter.

The *Northumberland* made it – only to go aground in the Hamoaze, that four-mile-long part of the estuary of the Tamar which has been the principal ship anchorage of Plymouth Harbour for generations of Royal Navy ships. The *Northumberland* was lucky. The *Harwich* was next in, and she didn't even make the Hamoaze. Captain Robinson of the *Harwich* realized his danger as the full strength of the wind hit him inside the Sound itself. He let go his anchors, but the strength of the wind and the ebb tide setting on shore made his wrecking certain. He was not helped in his attempts to keep off shore by the ships all around him which were doing their best to avoid the same fate. Despite all Captain Robinson's efforts, he was soon in only ten feet of water at his stern and 30 feet at the bow. Pumping and bailing had little effect, and she was quickly a wreck on the rocky shore. A wreck, but not a total loss. In that position a great deal of the ship, if not the whole ship, could be salvaged.

The *Royal Oak* at first seemed in even greater trouble. But luck was on her captain's side, and she finally ran aground fairly gently "under Mount Edgecumbe House" (and after being aground until September 9, was able to lift out her guns and be taken into the Dockyard for repairs).

The greatest tragedy was reserved for the last. Skelton brought his *Coronation* in exactly right for a run into the Sound through the deep western channel, but as he did so the wind increased and a gust caught her. She looked and felt as though she was going to capsize. The battering that she took then from the huge seas had started a massive leak below decks. The *Coronation* was seen to take on a savage list. Skelton realised his danger – later they were to say that he took in more water then as his gun-ports were not properly caulked or lined to keep out rough seas – and acted swiftly. His anchors went down. His masts were now the danger, accentuating the list until *Coronation* felt as though she was about to turn turtle under his feet. His orders were trumpeted into the teeth of a full gale, and the ship's carpenters sprang to their task. Within moments the great masts toppled down; they did not need cutting right through before snapping under their own weight.

Skelton may not yet have believed he was lost. His masts had gone, but he was still afloat with his ensign staff standing. But he was still listing. The end followed swiftly. One moment *Coronation* was there amid the white spume, the wind tearing off the tops of the waves; the next she rolled and was gone. Gone with her was Skelton and 600 men. It was a terrible tragedy, ranking top in the list of losses in any one shipwreck of the Royal Navy of those times. It shocked the town of Plymouth, and when it became known it shocked the country too. It even shocked Henry Greenhill, the Port Agent at Plymouth for the Commissioners of the Admiralty. But Henry Greenhill, being a pompous, miserable, mean man, did not think to start off with the loss of the *Coronation* in the letter he wrote to the Commissioners on September 4, 1691:

"May it Please Your Honours, I have received yours of the 1st instant and shall furnish Captain Evans with what Stores shall be needful for his Ship, if they are in Stores or can be procured and am glad that you are satisfied of the injustice of his late complaints. I have written Mss. Lowes of Bideford whom I employed to hire the vessel for Kinsale to send me a Certificate of the Agreement, which shall be transmitted to you in Order to you making out a Bill for the same.

"Yesterday our Fleete was forced into this Harbour by a Violent Storme of wind att S:S:East, the Coronation was unfortunately lost between the Rame Head and Pen Lee Point having first cut all her Masts by ye Board, most of the third rate made for the Hammoze where about Three or Four of them went ashore and the Harwich oversett, but the rest are or will all gett off Shore with little damage.

"The Admiral hath directed me to supply such Ships as have

received Damage with what is of absolute necessity for enabling them to go up this River, which we are now about and shall use the best husbandry possible and be as spareing as we can, though I fear this unhappy disaster will draw from Us a considerable quantity of Stores.

"It is now reported that the Sovereign and the Dutchesse are come into the Sound, who before were missing, and several other English and most of the Dutch Ships have as yett no notice of, and suppose they did not beare away with the Fleete, but there is a rumour of their being in Torbay, God grant itt may prove true.

"I beg your pardon for not giving you this Account by Express sent Last night to the Admiralty, having been on board the Elizabeth and other Ships all ye afternoone in wind and raine till late att night and greatly fatigued.

Your honoured and most humble Servant

Henry Greenhill

Plymouth ye 4th September
1691

There was about 22 of ye Seamen belonging to ye Coronation saved in their longboat and drove ashore upon some of ye Wreck, the Capn and Coll. Laston both drowned.

"P.S. Since writeing the foregoing I understand that ye James Gally and Portsmouth are come in and have brought with them a Privateer of 14 Gunns they afterwards fell with 4 French Greenland men, Very Strong who engaged them in which engagement Captain Bridges lost his right Arme. I have not yet spoken with the Commanders and therefore cannot give you a more particular Account."

There is little more detail to be found of the sinking. The various logbooks of the ships in the Fleet contain such reports as: "We lett goe both bower and sheate anchor in 20 fathom of water. When we were brought up our ship was about half of a mile from ye Ramehead ...Ye Coronation sank within two cables of us." And the court-martial throws only a little more light on it. It was held on board HMS *Duchess* on Thursday October 22, 1691. President of the court was Sir John Ashby, Vice-Admiral of the Red. His fellow judges in the great stern cabin of the *Duchess* were all Captains – Jones, Nevill, Lestock, Bokenham, Gother,

Hoskins, Edwards, Waters and Baker. And in careful, swirling copperplate writing, the clerk quilled that "all duly sworn persuant to a Late Act of Parliament concerning the Commissioners of ye Admiralty".

First matter to be dealt with was the loss of the *Harwich*, and after hearing all the facts, the court "did discharge and acquit Captain Henry Robinson and all the rest of ye Officers belonging to ye same". Then came the case of Skelton and the *Coronation*. The clerk's sharpened quill squeaked steadily on:

"Also enquiry was made concerning the losse of their Majesties late ship ye Coronation, which was oversett off ye Ramhead on ye Coast of Cornwall. Resolved, that the opinion of ye Court is, that by a Butt-head starting, or some Planke giving way Shee sprung a Leake, and thereby was lost. And doe not find that there was any Neglect or failure of Duty in Captain Skelton, Late Commander of ye sd Ship ye Coronation, or any of the officers belonging to ye same.

"Allso itt appears to ye Court that Mr. William Passinger Lately 1st Lieutenant of ye Coronation, was absent from ye sd Ship by his Captain's Order, being sent to Falmouth for water and fresh provisions, and therfore the Court does discharge and acquit the sd Mr. Passinger, as to what relates to ye losse of ye Ship Coronation."

And that it seemed was that. The *Coronation* had gone down in deep water. The bodies which were washed up amid wooden wreckage all along the coast were buried where they came ashore. And no one even thought of salvage. The Admiralty had other things to worry about – HMS *Exeter*, of 70 guns, was accidentally blown up in Plymouth Harbour on September 12, and the French had still to be beaten at sea. So the Navy got on with the war and the *Coronation's* loss was, if not forgotten, soon only something for old salts to recall.

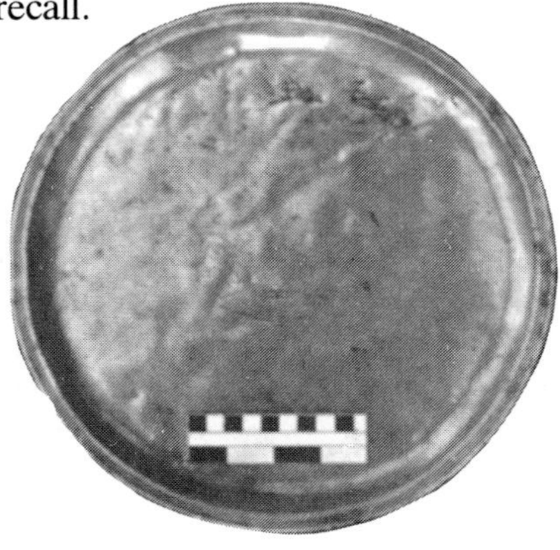

Pewter plate bearing the crest of Charles Skelton

Diving the Coronation

A diver from Alan Bax's team over a 'Coronation' cannon.

THE WRECK SITE of the *Coronation* is in two parts; one offshore is officially the *Coronation*, and the other inshore is unidentified, but everyone knows that it is really the *Coronation* too. The inshore site was discovered in 1967 by Plymouth Sound divers Terry Harrison, Alan Down and George Sandford when they first of all spotted some cannonballs. A trail of these led them in close to Lady Island, Penlee Point, where in less than 10 metres were cannon. Lots of cannon. They finally counted 40 of them. In 1968 the Plymouth divers introduced Lt-Commander Alan Bax, R.N. to the site. Bax, a leading member of the Committee for Nautical Archaeology, protected the site by taking out a lease of the seabed of the area around the cannon. And that lease is still in force. This means that though divers can dive on the site, they must touch nothing unless they are taking part in an archaeological survey of the site.

The cannon site was surveyed and other items discovered, such as big bronze pulley wheels which bore the Navy's broad arrow mark, but even though this was more evidence of the loss of a large Navy ship, there was no evidence that could actually prove that it was the last resting place of *Coronation*, even though she was the only ship lost in the area which would fit the discoveries.

In 1977 underwater archaeologist Peter McBride carried out a magnetometer search and got a very strong contact about half-a mile off Lady Island. Diving the spot produced 16 cannon and several large anchors, and an amazing piece of luck in the shape of a pewter plate. The maker's mark on it was identified as that of James Tisoe of Westminster whose stamp dates back to 1689. There was a horse's head crest on the plate too, and it proved to be that of the Skelton family. It also explained why young Charles got off to such a good start early in his naval career. He was very well-connected, a son of the Lieutenant-Governor of Plymouth and brother of Sir Bevill Skelton, a diplomat and Groom of the Bedchamber to Charles II. As a result of the plate's discovery this site became the official grave of *Coronation* and was designated as a historic wreck. Today diving is not allowed within 150 metres of a point given in the designation order as 50 18.57; 04 11.98 W.

There can be little doubt that this is the place where *Coronation* "oversett", dumping part of her contents on the seabed before drifting away later to deposit most of the rest in the shallows amid the kelp near Lady Island on Penlee Point. A recovery from this

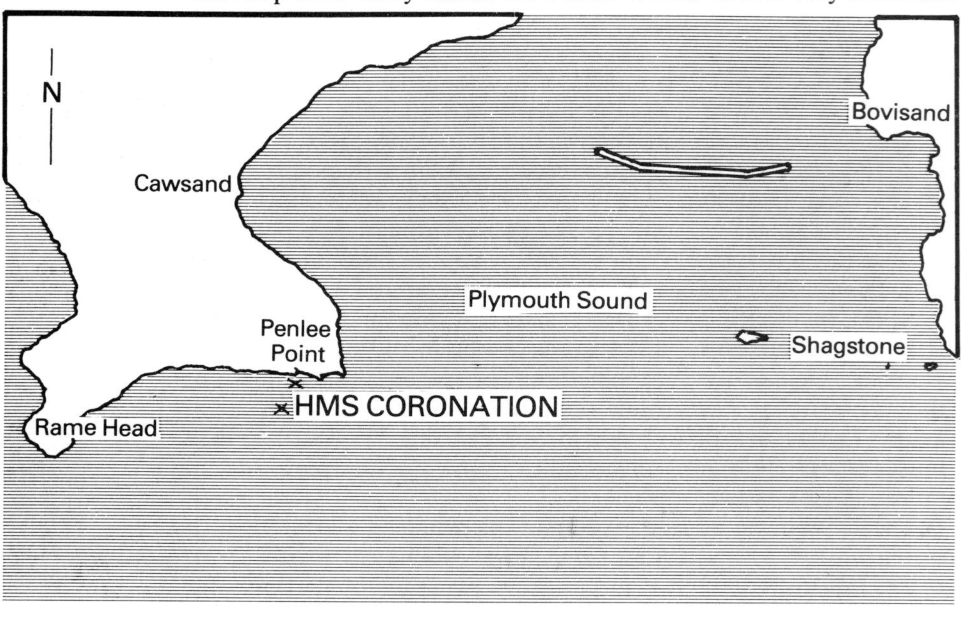

inshore site which was almost a clincher of its identity, but again not quite, came in 1980 when a diver found a sword handle near Penlee Point. It was identical to one which had been found offshore on the official *Coronation* site. Both sword handles bore a lion's head and were of the type of short swords or "hangers" worn by members of gun crews in Naval ships of the period. Later, another similar sword handle was found near Lady Island. In 1983 an extensive survey was carried out on and close to the Penlee Point site. This expedition was led by Mark Fuller and Peter Bernardes, and an additional 24 cannon were found. This brings the total of cannon from both sites to 83, just seven short of *Coronation's* 90 guns.

All those who have dived the inshore site believe there is much more to be found in the area. Somewhere on the seabed no doubt is an artefact which will prove that *Coronation* is in two places at once. Divers in the area should keep an eye open for any such material and report it to Alan Bax at Fort Bovisand Underwater Centre, just across the Sound from the Penlee site. Fort Bovisand is the place to obtain air, and the ramp there provides an easy safe launch for small boats to explore the Penlee site at 50 19 00; 04 11 30W.

Forty 'Coronation' cannons were found in an area surveyed off Penlee Point.

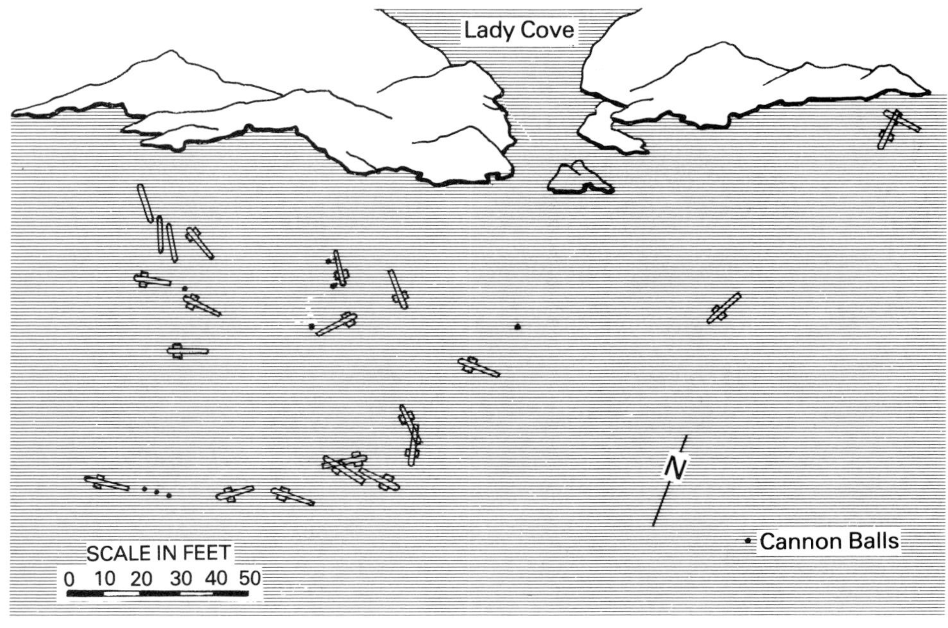

Coronation wreck log

Position: 50 19 00; 04 11 30W.

Penlee Point, Cornwall

Chart No.: 1613

Date: ....

Dive leader: ....

Equipment used:
ABLJ/STAB .... Air capacity: ....

Suit... Demand valve ....

Weights: .... SMB/reel ....

Special equipment ....

Dive Boat:...

Weather..........................Sea Height...........State of tide...........

Current ....Underwater viz ....

Dive timing:
Left surface ....Returned surface..........................

Maximum depth:...

Decompression required...

Seabed type............................Scour present ....

State of wreckage ....

Area of ship dived: ....

Special points to note: ....

....

CHAPTER FOUR

The Louis Sheid

THOUGH NO TORPEDO ran within miles of her, the *Louis Sheid* was sunk by a U-boat as surely as if she had been hit full amidships. For it was fear of the *U-47* which sent the *Sheid* running in to the shelter of the coast and into shallow water where

her captain hoped no U-boat would dare to follow. Unfortunately, he took her in too close. The captain of the *Louis Sheid* was quite right to fear a U-boat attack on his ship in those early months of the war, for loose in the Channel was Korvettenkapitan Gunther Prien, who was sinking any ship which came his way. And it made no difference to Prien if his targets were neutral ships. Whether this was a slavish devotion to his orders, or whether the adulation accorded to him as Germany's first hero of World War Two had gone to his head it is impossible to say. But Prien was certainly a brave man and a good submarine commander. He had been decorated by Hitler with the Knights Cross With Oak Leaves for sinking the Royal Navy's 29 000-ton battleship *Royal Oak* at anchor in Scapa Flow only two months

U-boat commander Gunther Prien (left) receives congratulations from a German naval chief.

earlier. The *Royal Oak* sank in 13 minutes on October 14, 1939, with the loss of 833 lives.

Now Prien had been unleashed again into the Allied shipping lanes. In the early morning of December 7, 1939, he had found another target, and was lining up on her despite the fact that her markings clearly showed her to be Dutch, and at that time a neutral. Prien had come from humble circumstances in Leipzig, but had managed to attend a nautical school in Hamburg, which passed him out as a fourth officer. In the Great Depression he became unemployed. He entered the German Navy in 1932 as a warrant officer, and was commissioned the next year. At the outbreak of war he was commanding *U-47* and it was in this boat that he sank the *Royal Oak*.

It was through the periscope of *U-47* on December 7 that Prien prepared to attack the Dutch ship. She was the 8159-ton Dutch cargo-liner *Tajandoen*, bound from Amsterdam for Batavia with 14 passengers and a general cargo of cement, iron, steel sheet, glassware, aniline and pharmaceutical goods of many kinds. He lined up on her at 5.24 am, and hit her with one torpedo full in her port side at 5.30. The Dutch ship began to sink almost at once. The explosion of the torpedo was heard clearly on the *Louis Sheid*, homeward bound for Antwerp with a cargo of grain and a crew of 46. The *Louis Sheid* was neutral. She was a big ship of 6057 tons, 418 feet long, with a beam of 55 feet, but was not new. She had in fact been built by Nord Werft of Wesermunde for the Rickmers Line in 1920. She was launched as the *Ultor*. When she was taken over by the James Chambers Lancashire Shipping Line of Liverpool they renamed her the *Kendal Castle*. Another take-over by the Belgian National Shipping Line gave her the name of *Louis Sheid*. And so there was no doubt about her neutrality at the outbreak of war the word "BELGIE" was painted in huge white letters on her sides and, to stress the point, outlined in white beside the lettering was an even larger Belgian flag. If Britain was at war with Germany, Belgium was definitely not.

It is much to the credit of the captain and men of the *Louis Sheid* that she immediately headed for the stricken ship, even though they must have guessed she was the victim of a submarine and that submarine was likely to be still close by. In fact Prien had headed away as soon as he heard his torpedo strike. Which was lucky for the *Louis Sheid* – and for the survivors of the *Tajandoen*. The torpedo strike had split the Dutch ship's fuel tanks, and fuel swirled on the surface all around her. Only six of the crew failed to reach the lifeboats before they were lowered, and it is believed that they were killed in the explosion of the torpedo. The 62 men who did get into the boats had no sooner done so than the fuel oil around the ship ignited. But they rowed madly across the blazing sea, and finally, in blackened boats, scorched and singed, managed to reach the safety of the *Louis Sheid.*

Once the captain of the *Sheid* had the survivors safely aboard, he knew he too might share the Dutch ship's fate. Prien and *U-47* were obviously no respecters of neutrality, and picking up survivors might well be construed by such a U-boat commander, if he so wished, as a hostile act. So the *Louis Sheid* ran for the nearest land and inshore waters where the U-boat might not dare to go. By nightfall she was running close in to the South Devon coast. Soon a Southerly gale and heavy rain squalls were blotting out the shape of the land. Due to the blackout regulations there were no friendly shore-lights to tell the captain that he was standing right in to danger. He missed the rocks they call The Delvers, which reach out from Warren Point, and came right into the tiny bay called Leas Foot, near the clubhouse of Thurlestone Golf Club. On the South side of the little beach of Leas Foot, another tiny headland with a small reef at its foot was waiting. And there the *Louis Sheid* struck, just as the tide was dropping. She was not only almost on the golf course, but she was also only a few hundred feet from the Links Hotel, which is now converted into a block of flats and called Links Court. As a result she did not strand unnoticed. In fact Jack Jarvis, the former cox'n of the old Hope Cove lifeboat saw it happen and phoned Salcombe.

The Salcombe lifeboat, the *Samuel and Mary Parkhouse*, was away in minutes – beam to in the same Southerly gale that had pushed the *Louis Sheid* on to the rocks. The lifeboat had a hellish journey around the Bolt and, in enormous seas, finally found the ship two hours later. The *Louis Sheid* had her engines at full speed, but it was almost Low Water, and it made no difference. The ship was firmly on the rocks. The Salcombe lifeboat men anchored off and lowered themselves back on to her. Finally, on her port side, they found some shelter and got a rope on to the Belgian steamer. But it was no comfortable position. The lifeboat was rising and falling nearly 30 feet as wave followed wave, and as each man jumped into the lifeboat he had to be caught and steadied by a member of the crew and got out of the way ready for the next man to take advantage of the upswing. And it was only after 40 men had got aboard in this way that the lifeboat cox'n

Overleaf: crowds surround the rocket apparatus as the crew of the 'Louis Sheid' is rescued by the line it fired.

BELGIE

Eddie Distin found that he was rescuing not one crew, but two. All the first 40 men came from the *Tajandoen*!

The lifeboat couldn't cope with so many all at once. It made two trips, taking off all the Dutchmen and landing them with great difficulty at Hope Cove. Local fishermen dared enormous waves to set up a ferry service from lifeboat to shore. When the Salcombe lifeboat returned for the third time, the *Louis Sheid* had been moved by the wind and seas and the rising tide. She was now jammed broadside on under the cliffs and in the dawn it was clear that she was unlikely to sail again. Already she was starting to show signs of heavy damage. The rocket apparatus was set up on the cliff overlooking her and got a line aboard; later all the crew came off safely. Cox'n Eddie Distin was awarded the RNLI Silver Medal for the rescue and each of his crew, the Bronze.

THE LOUIS SHEID

They tried hard in the next few months to move the Belgian ship, but all attempts failed. Soon she started to show signs of extensive damage. Some of her grain was salvaged, but the rest formed fizzy mounds along nearby beaches. The salvage teams moved in to take what could be used again, but in 1940 South-Westerly gales broke her in two. More salvage was tried in 1942, and on April 29 that year the Salcombe lifeboat was called out again to save eight of the salvage crew from a small boat which had stranded on the Books Rocks in an East-South-Easterly gale. That year most of the bow collapsed, but salvage work went on in fits and starts and at one time an aerial ropeway was set up to the wreck from the cliffs and driven by a traction engine. Lots of metal was cut off her. Later still, after the war, she was sold for £400 and more salvage took place.

The 'Louis Sheid' broken by the gales of 1940.

Gunther Prien did not survive long. He was killed on March 8, 1941, when his *U-47* was depth-charged by the destroyer HMS *Wolverine* and exploded under water. There were no survivors.

Diving the Louis Sheid

APPROACH THURLESTONE by taking the A381 out of Kingsbridge, following signposts for Salcombe. Immediately after leaving the town and climbing up the hill through West Alvington (*take care* – very narrow) branch right following signposts to Thurlestone. Now a very narrow lane, with passing places, takes you to the B3197. Turn right at T-junction, continue to first decent turning on left (signposted "Thurlestone") and follow straight on to the little thatched village of Thurlestone. Keep right on through the village, past the Village Inn and the Church, down to Thurlestone Golf Clubhouse on your right. Turn right across face of clubhouse. Do not park in spaces in front of clubhouse – reserved for officials! The road you are now in is a dead end due to coast erosion. On your right is the little beach of Leas Foot.

It is possible to get an inflatable across the beach, but it can be a hard haul over soft sand. Do not leave your car there, but take it back past the clubhouse and park in the large car park just before the main road. The small headland on your left as you face the sea is the grave of the *Louis Sheid*. She is among the rocks of the small reef which reaches out from that headland at 50 15 48; 03 52 12 W. At low tide you will see her stempost stick up out of the water. It is a reasonable distance to snorkel out to her. She is in 10m of water amid kelp on rock. The boilers are still there and they house some of the largest wrasse I have seen on this section of the coast. Many ribs are still clear. In early Summer you will find a good number of spider crabs on them and on the rest of the wreckage, which mainly consists of steel plate here, there and everywhere.

This wreck-dive is one of the best introductions to wreck-diving for beginners that I know. A boat is not essential, but does add to the pleasure of diving the clear, usually calm waters over the wreck. The easiest place to launch an inflatable is the far end of

THE LOUIS SHEID

Thurlestone Sands, where there is easy access and plentiful car-parking behind the beach. However, you cannot drive directly from Leas Foot to Thurlestone Sands. To get there you must return to the A381 and take the turning marked "Thurlestone Sands", much further on towards Salcombe, or go via South Milton. Air is available in Kingsbridge from Kingsbridge Watersports, 39 Fore Street. Tel: Kingsbridge (0548) 2934.

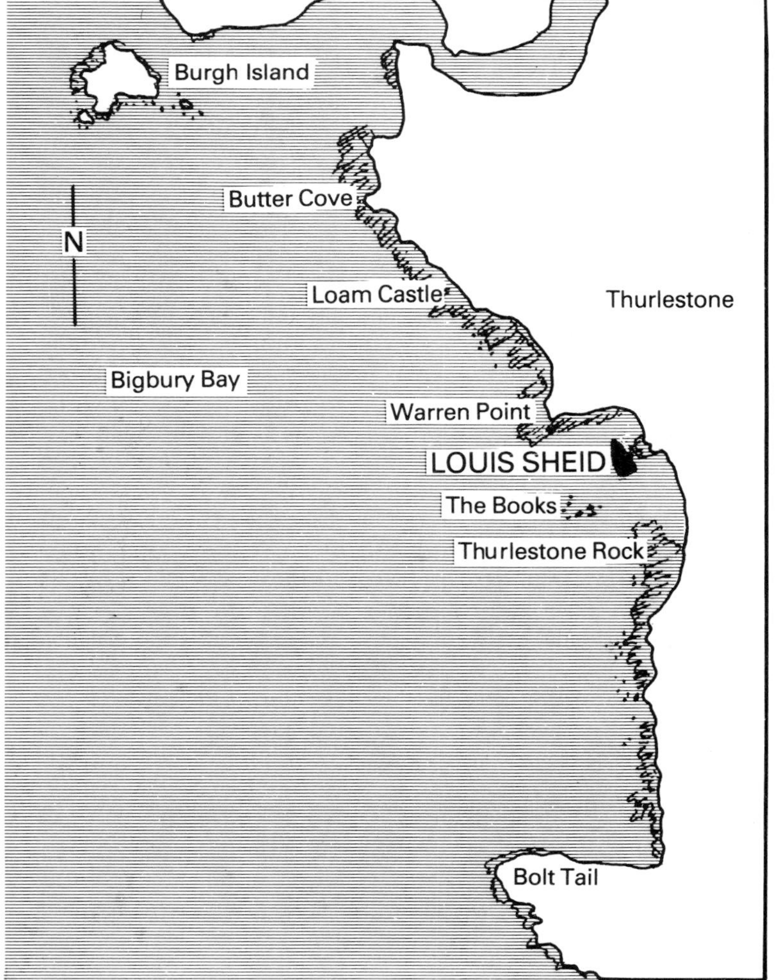

The 'Louis Sheid' lies in 10 metres of water on a reef off the beach of Leas Foot.

Louis Sheid wreck log

Position: 50 15 48; 03 52 12W.

Leas Foot, Thurlestone, Devon

Chart No.: 1613

Date: ....

Dive leader: ....

Equipment used:
ABLJ/STAB .... Air capacity: ....

Suit.. Demand valve ....

Weights: .... SMB/reel ....

Special equipment ....

Dive Boat: ....

Weather............................Sea Height............State of tide............

Current ....Underwater viz ....

Dive timing:
Left surface ....Returned surface...........................

Maximum depth:...

Decompression required..

Seabed type..............................Scour present ....

State of wreckage ....

Area of ship dived: ....

Special points to note: ....

....

....

....

....

....

....

....

....

....

....

CHAPTER FIVE

HMS Pine

AS WARS GO, it was quiet in the English Channel at the end of January, 1944. Not that you could ever call the Channel really quiet in World War Two, and certainly not in the parts of it which were narrow enough to have earned the nickname of "E-boat Alley". But on January 30, 1944, the Home Command entry in the "Most Secret" sections of the War Diary did seem to be fairly peaceful. As wars go. On page 500, for example, there were important details of British submarine movements. *Sceptre* and

Satyr and *Spirit* were all on the move from outside Muckle Flugga in the Shetlands to Lerwick – and to avoid any unfortunate cases of mistaken identity, they were all travelling submerged during daylight hours. *Tradewind* and *Trusty* were taking the same precautions though they were outward bound. Logged next were almost routine reports ... Four British MTB's had been shelled by German shore batteries near Fecamp ... "Operation Bellpush" (whatever that was) had been "partially successful" ... A German air raid on Brightlingsea had caused minor damage by incendiaries to the Blackwater Naval Station ... The trawler *Ply* had been attacked by a Junkers 88 20 miles South by West of Fastnet. The next entry concerned convoy movements in the Channel and said that Convoy C.W.243 had set out from Southend at 1100 hours and the 19 ships were coming steadily down Channel at seven knots. Then a piece of excitement! An aircraft of Coastal Command reported being over a German U-boat at 59 33 00; 13 46 00 West, but the U-boat submerged

HMS Pine's sister ship, the Bay.

MOST SECRET

Enclosure to Portsmouth No. 880/0/0205/45/486 of 15th February 1944.

FROM...THE COMMANDING OFFICER, H.M.S.ALBRIGHTON.

DATE...FEBRUARY 4, 1944. Ref No. ALB/ops/7.

TO.....THE COMMANDER IN CHIEF, PORTSMOUTH. (Copy to THE CAPTAIN(D), FIRST DESTROYER FLOTILLA.)

Subject. Report of Battle.

Submitted:-

Nature of Action - Attack by E-boats on Convoy C.W. 243, 30/31 January, 1944.

2. Disposition of Escorts - Ref. Eastern Channel Convoy Instructions page 6.

Destroyers (Albrighton (S.O.) D.6.
(Quorn D.2.

M.L's. 206 - L.1. 185 - L.11.
207 - L.2. 464 - L.12.
597 - L.6. 589 - Link.

Minesweepers. WALNUT. (S.O.) S.3.
BLACKTHORN. S.2.
PINE. S.1.

3. Convoy - Consisted of 19 ships in two columns led by the Commodore in H.M.S.Haslemere and leading the Port column. 2 Rescue vessels H.M.Trawlers "REHEARO" and "LORRAINE", sailed at the rear of each column.

4. Weather - Ideal for E-boat attack - Calm sea, slight sou'westerly breeze, strata cloud forming up from the South at 1000 - 1500 feet, 3/10 at 0100 and 10/10 by 0400.

5. Narrative -

2100 - Naval proceedure heard on 'Headache', very loud, units being tuned in, a maneuvering signal, followed by an order to close down watch. 6 E-boat and 2 R-boat call signs were identified. Convoy was in the vicinity of S.W.Gate Buoy, Dover Channel, at this time. In error I considered this to be an Escort Force probably operating from Calais to the Northward

0026 - Moon had set and shaded stern lights could be seen in the Convoy. I ordered "Show no lights".

immediately, and the Sunderland lost contact. The Wren compiling the War Diary typed steadily on as each message was handed to her. Now the date changed. It was Monday, January 31, 1944. Out at sea in the dark of the Channel, Convoy C.W. 243 steamed steadily on in two columns, with three armed trawlers a mile and threequarters ahead of them minesweeping the way clear. It was all very quiet, but Convoy C.W. 243 was soon to make its own large entry in the War Diary. They were, after all, to go through E-boat Alley.

HMS PINE

In a Sussex coast radar station just after midnight, it was quiet too. The screen showed the 19 blips of the convoy which hardly seemed to move as sweep followed sweep. On the merchant ships' port bow was the destroyer HMS *Quorn*. The armed trawlers HMS *Rehearo* and HMS *Lorraine* brought up the rear of each column. The convoy commodore in HMS *Haslemere*, a Fleet auxiliary, was leading the port column of merchant ships. To the rear of the whole convoy was another destroyer, HMS *Albrighton*, and screening the seaward side of the convoy were six well-armed motor launches. Within easy calling distance were more Navy ships, a flotilla of MTB's, ready, willing and able to mix it with any attack from their high-speed counterparts in German E-boats. With all this fire-power to hand, the men in the merchant ships felt reasonably secure, but even so were careful to keep their stations in the middle of the protective screen. On board HMS *Albrighton* her Captain, Lieutenant John Hooker, did not share the merchantmen's complete confidence in their safety. Just minutes into the new day he had made a note in the log that conditions were ideal for an E-boat attack: "Calm sea, slight sou'westerly breeze, strata cloud forming up from the South at 1000–1500 feet, 3/10".

By 26 minutes past midnight, the moon had set, but visibility was still good. As the moonlight faded, shaded stern lights could be seen in the convoy ahead of his ship. Hooker knew well that the Masters of some merchant ships still held the opinion that stern lights were necessary for station keeping on dark nights, but it was always stressed at convoy conferences, and had been this time, that good station keeping can be kept on a darkened ship provided the ships remained well closed up. So he ordered "Show no lights!" and was relieved to see the lights go out. About the same time his "Headache" set crackled into life – "Headache" was the code-name for a radio operation with German-speaking operators who could listen in to German Naval signals. Now the

Opposite: extract from John Hooker's log.

German voices were very loud, and six E-boats and two other torpedo boats could be heard netting in to one another. Hooker guessed that this was a German escort force well to the North, and probably operating from Calais. He was right about Calais, but wrong about the escort idea. Escort duty was the furthest thing from the Germans' minds – what he had heard was in fact a force of ten E-boats tuning in their radios before setting out after him and his convoy C.W.243. At 0145 there were sounds on his Asdic, but it seemed to be coming from one of the escort motor launches.

At precisely the same moment, the radar operator on the Sussex shore could hardly believe what his eyes were telling him. Racing across his screen at nearly 40 knots straight towards the plodding seven-knot blips of the convoy were ten new plots. A plot travelling at that speed and on that course could only mean one thing – that German E-boats were loose in the Channel and closing in for the kill. Consolation for the convoy was all that fire-power around it, and it only needed a warning from the coast radar station to put it all into protective action. The radar operator did his part. The warning was drafted, timed at 0148 and marked with the one word "Immediate". But that is as far as it got. The next step should have been for a civilian operator to transmit the signal with all urgency. But such a thing had never happened to him before – in training yes, but never for real – and as he didn't want to make any mistake, he decided to go by the book. And the book said that such a plain language transmission needed the authorisation of a senior Naval officer. But there wasn't such a creature on the station at that moment. So, as the civilian operator picked up the telephone to ask for permission elsewhere, the countdown to disaster had begun.

At 0150 starshell and tracer arced away to the South and Hooker knew that it came from *Quorn*. Two minutes later starshells soared up from *Albrighton* herself. In their light in harsh outline were two E-boats, clearly heading for the convoy. In the bright light, they made smoke and turned away to the East. Now it seemed that each starshell, no matter who fired it, silhouetted E-boats all round. But as soon as the light hit them, the flickering outlines ringed in the white spray of speed, weaved, made smoke and disappeared behind it. *Albrighton* was at speed too, engaging each target as it appeared, sending 17 four-inch shells and 42 two-pounder rounds at the high-speed twisting shapes. Once a big flash on board one of the E-boats looked like a clear hit, but the boat continued its run as though completely unhurt. Later,

Hooker believed that the flash was a torpedo being fired from one of the E-boats right at him!

Ahead of the convoy, the three armed trawlers were plugging along at 7.7 knots in a star formation, with their starboard sweeps out. HMS *Pine* was on the starboard side, HMS *Blackthorn* to port, and HMS *Walnut* was slightly in the lead in the centre. Captain of *Walnut* was Lt-Commander Hamilton Adams, RNVR, who was in command, too, of the three anti-submarine mine-sweeping trawlers for this convoy operation. Each of his charges was rated as 530 tons, carried a 12-pounder gun, as well as two 0.5-inch anti-aircraft guns and two twin Lewis machine guns. It hardly needed Commander Adams to give the command "Action stations"; it was quite clear to the mine-sweepers that the convoy behind them was under attack. They were not to be left out of the main action for long. At 0205 Commander Adams felt a massive explosion on his starboard side. *Walnut* was making smoke at the time, and that, together with the darkness, meant that his view astern was nil. When the smoke cleared, he could only see HMS *Blackthorn*. HMS *Pine* had disappeared. A moment later a lookout spotted an E-boat moving away from his port side out to sea. Adams ordered starshells to be fired, but the E-boat had got away. Moments later he intercepted a message from the escort commander to the convoy commodore that a trawler had been torpedoed in the van of the convoy, and he knew exactly what had happened to HMS *Pine*.

In fact *Pine* never saw the E-boat which sank her. The torpedo came out of the dark and blew her bows almost completely off. Ten of the 37 men on board died at once, but the trawler didn't sink, despite her severe damage, and wallowed to a standstill on the calm sea as the main body of the convoy overtook her. As they did so Lieutenant-Commander Henry Leslie, commanding the First Motor Launch Flotilla from *M.L.206* put his ship alongside the battered *Pine* and took off 20 survivors. Henry Leslie had heard an underwater explosion just before finding the *Pine*, followed by an escape of steam. At the same time he had seen the stern light of one of the mine-sweepers go out. He closed the *Pine* by using his radar, and formed a quick opinion that the trawler was unlikely to sink swiftly, and decided to stand by her. At that moment – 0209 in the wireless office in HMS *Albrighton* – they logged in the radar station's warning of E-boats approaching. The civilian had finally found his senior Naval Officer and the necessary permission. Later, Lieutenant Hooker, RN noted sure. Now in view of 'Headache' received at 0210 I think that a torpedo was fired probably at "Quorn", were she at this time in the position estimated by my plot.

0208 -(approx) Two underwater explosions in quick succession reported by Asdic. A flash and shower of sparks seen to the W.N.W.

0209 -N.O.I.C.[redacted] 0148 received in my W/T Office. Delay in receipt of this vital information was disastrous.

Hooker's note about the delayed warning.

grimly beside the entry: "Delay in receipt of this vital information was disastrous."

It was. Some of the E-boats, which were hunting in small groups, were now in amongst the convoy and were attacking the columns of ships from both sides. *Quorn* and *Albrighton* raced along at 20 knots, fending off attacks, but the E-boats' skilful use of speed and of smoke screens made more casualties a foregone conclusion. At 0214 the 806-ton s.s. *Emerald*, the second ship in the port column, laden with coal and heading from Middlesbrough to Poole, was hit by a torpedo. Almost immediately she listed to port and went down swiftly by the stern. She took her crew of 12 and three Naval gunners with her. A minute later it seemed that the E-boats had actually penetrated in between the convoy's lines, for a Norweigan ship the *Ara*, number three in the starboard column, fired her machine guns at a target running between the columns of British ships. And a minute later, the 1,813-ton s.s. *Caleb Sprague* took a torpedo in her engine room on the port side. Amid a shower of sparks, the mainmast came down, and the ship's back broke just astern of the engine room. She went down with bow and stern both sticking up in the air. Of the crew of 31 which included four Naval gunners, only seven survived the sinking. One of those survivors was the Chief Officer, Mr. A.H. Mackie, who was exceptionally lucky, as he was asleep at the time of the torpedo striking. Later he told this dramatic story of the events of that January night:

"We were bound from Southend to Newport, Mon., with a cargo of 2305 tons of steel and timber, and were mainly armed with one four-inch and a Lewis gun. The crew numbered 31, including four Naval gunners. Of this number 24 are missing. The seven survivors were myself, one AB, Gunner Hulme, Cook, Bo'sun, Radio Operator and Second Officer. The Second Officer was injured and died on board the rescuing trawler. All confidential books, which were kept in the chart room in a weighted box, went down with the ship. We left Southend at 1100 on the 30th of January in Convoy C.W.243, which formed up in two columns outside "D" Buoy. Our position was fourth ship in the starboard column. The convoy proceeded without incident until 0200 on 31st January, 1944, when in position 10 miles

South-East from Beachy Head, steering West-North-West at a speed of seven knots, we were struck by one torpedo from an E-boat. There was a calm sea, slight swell, with light airs. The weather was fine, visibility good.

"No one in my ship saw the E-boat. The Radio Operator, who was standing at the after end of the boat deck at the time, said that he saw flares and the ship ahead fired her machine guns a few seconds before we were struck. The torpedo hit on the port side, in the engine room, with a violent explosion. I was in my room and saw nothing, but the Radio Operator told me later that he saw a mass of sparks and a huge column of water thrown up and the mainmast collapse. I was awakened by the explosion, which vibrated in my ears. I jumped off my settee, seized my lifejacket and rushed out on deck to find the ship already sinking beneath me. I was taken down as she sank, which could not have been more than 15 seconds after the explosion. I swam to the surface and momentarily saw the bows of the ship not far from me. I could not see her stern. It appeared that the ship had broken in two abaft the engine room, with the two ends rising in the air as she sank.

"I swam desperately to clear the suction, which was so strong that I felt I was in the middle of a whirlpool, until I found myself alongside a large piece of timber which probably came from No.2 hold. I put this under my arms for extra support and another piece of timber which floated by under my knees. I was wearing my lifejacket. After a few minutes I heard a shout and recognised the voice of one of the AB's. I called back and he told me he was hanging on to a lifebelt box. I switched on the red light on my lifejacket, which worked efficiently, and waited to be picked up. I saw no other survivors in the water."

Mr. Mackie was to wait for nearly an hour before being picked up by the trawler HMS *Rehearo*, and in the meantime the battle moved on. But the E-boats almost appeared satisfied with their three "kills" for soon after the *Caleb Sprague* went down they broke off the action. For some time the convoy commander expected a further attack, and ordered his charges to "hug the coast". But the E-boats had gone almost as swiftly as they had come. They had suffered no loss, and clearly regarded the action as a considerable victory. The whole thing had lasted just half an hour. Though both British merchant ships had sunk swiftly after being torpedoed, *Pine* was still afloat, and Lt-Commander Leslie close by in *M.L.206* now thought she could be saved. But first he had a more urgent task. The *Pine's* 20 survivors, whom he already had on board, insisted that there were likely to be more men alive on board her. Some, they said, had stayed at their posts below, even after she was hit, and not all of them were accounted for. So Leslie went back alongside *Pine* and sent off a boarding party to search the shattered ship. They found another seven men alive.

Commander Leslie now found himself alone, left behind by all the convoy, but expecting one of the armed trawlers which had sailed in a rescue role at the rear of each column to appear at any minute in response to his signals and take the *Pine* in tow. But nothing happened. Leslie ignored an earlier message to rejoin the convoy, believing, rightly, that his signals were not being heard. From reading all the signals traffic of the action, Lt-Cmdr. Leslie appears to have been an extremely forceful young man. It was clear that he risked further attack by the E-boats, but he would

not leave the *Pine*. In fact it was not until 0340 that the trawler, HMS *Rehearo*, which had been picking up survivors from the *Caleb Sprague*, was in the words of Leslie's report "sighted, closed and ordered to take Pine in tow".

Pine was towed towards Beachy Head and the safety of Newhaven. But though Leslie took his motor launch into Newhaven at 0814 and disembarked the *Pine's* survivors, his dealings with the damaged trawler were not complete. The Naval Officer in Command, Newhaven, ordered the *Pine* to be towed by the inshore route to Portsmouth, where there were better repair facilities, and the tug *Resolve*, escorted by one motor launch, took over the tow at 0859 that morning. Two of the *Pine's* surviving officers asked to be put back on board their ship, and Leslie's motor launch was detailed to do this. He left Newhaven at 1015 and overtook the *Pine*, placing the officers on board at 1215. They

An E-boat at full throttle.

were not to be back on their old ship for long – at 1325, when Selsey Bill was just six miles awy, HMS *Pine* suddenly sank.

The Germans clearly regarded the action as highly successful. We know that not only because of British losses but because on board one of the E-boats was a German radio war reporter, Hans Werner Kaemper, and when he regaled his German radio audience with the story of the mission against Convoy C.W.243, the BBC German radio monitoring service was listening. And this is how Herr Kaemper described it all.

"When we left harbour and saw the light mist and fog shrouding the coast, we did not believe in the success of the night ahead of us. Bad visibility is unfavourable to any operational activity at sea, but when we drew away from the coast, the fog and mist disappeared. The thin crescent of the moon threw her soft light on the long white trail of foam behind us. A convoy, hugging the British coast is to be our target. Shall we be successful this time? Shall we be able to get near the convoy despite the strong and numerous defences to be expected? When we are a few miles from the British coast, the different groups of ships of the flotilla part company. They will penetrate the convoy from different directions. Suddenly star shells astern!

"We hear the muffled sounds of the first salvoes greeting our comrades. It seems we have missed the tail end of the convoy and we now turn round to the battle area ... Suddenly we see a huge glow of fire over the horizon, quickly succeeded by a second one. Explosions follow, then everything is completely dark again. It seems our comrades have been successful! Now, however, the British defence increases. Star shell after star shell hang under the racing clouds. Soon we, too, have been spotted and must turn and twist. All around us are wildly patrolling motor gunboats. It must have been an hour or more that these attempts to get us lasted until our group of boats had to cease fighting as the time for which the return journey had been ordered was reached. We must content ourselves with our comrades' success.

"They had reached the British coast without encountering any defence, and they saw there in the glow of star shells intended for us and our comrades, the convoy only some hundred metres ahead of them. Two great steamers of 3,000 tons and 2,500 tons lie in front of them as if presented on a plate. The young Commander's decisions are short and quick. The boats turn their bows in the direction of the two steamers and soon the death-bringing torpedoes leave their tubes. The explosions follow after only a few seconds. In the bright glare of the explosions the two steamers break in two almost amidships. Bow and stern rise for the last time and then sink under the water while the boats hear the steam rushing from their engines. An escort vessel, which has not yet spotted the two German boats, comes in sight at the same moment. She may be about 400 to 500 gross tons. She is only some hundred metres away, and the torpedo is followed by the explosion within a few seconds; this escort vessel too sinks immediately..."

Dramatic stuff and even if the *Pine* did struggle some 40 miles from the scene of the attack before finally sinking, the E-boats did get right the number of ships they had sunk in their attack that January night in E-boat Alley. But would they have sunk three ships if that wireless operator at a Sussex radar station had sent the warning message as soon as he was given it? Would HMS *Pine* and *Caleb Sprague* and *Emerald* have survived the war if he had? About the loss of the *Pine* one man had no doubts. In the battle report which Lieutenant John Hooker, Commanding Officer of HMS *Albrighton*, sent to the Commander-in Chief, Portsmouth, with a copy to the Captain of the First Destroyer Flotilla, he wrote: "Had the Sussex signal of 0148 been received before 0155, actually not until 0209, it is thought that counter-action by the escorts might have been taken successfully to the attack on the front of the Convoy."

And of course he may well have been right. If the E-boat attack could have been harrassed by the escorts right from the start, the whole pattern of the action would have changed. It seems from conclusions drawn by the convoy commodore in his report of the action that he too considered the delay an important factor in the British losses. And he thought that the torpedoing of the *Pine* and the merchant ships was not part of the normal E-boat attack pattern and that most of the torpedoing was done from almost stationary E-boats. The attackers of C.W.243 came from the E-boat flotilla based at Calais. These boats in 1944 were the new 95-tonners with a length of 106 feet, driven by three diesels with a top speed of 46 knots. Their usual attack pattern was to set out in a flotilla of nine or ten and then to break into "Rotte" or groups of two or three and attack the convoy at full speed, retiring to reload torpedoes, a process which took about five minutes. The attack on C.W.243 seems from Herr Kaemper's radio report, and from the convoy commodore's own observations at the head of the merchant ships, to have been a much more leisurely affair, with

E-boats sitting waiting for the convoy to come to them instead of hurtling at it at high speed from out of the darkness. And with the proper warning that E-boat plan could have been broken up before it could have been put into operation. So it seems that the *Pine*, at least, might have been saved.

Diving HMS Pine

THOSE WHO WOULD dive the *Pine* should check before doing so that she has not been designated under the Military Remains Protection Act of 1986. In view of the fact that all casualties were removed from her before she was taken under tow from Newhaven, such protection is unlikely, but you never know. Today, she is at 50 43 05; 00 37 10. Her 164-foot hull is well broken, as she is very shallow – 10 metres at Low, and never more than 20m at High. It is fair to describe her now as a good "rummage" dive over a very wide area. At one time she was used by many of the Littlehampton dive boats as a good second dive after a deep one further out, but they now tend to find that the tide times don't fit with their long trips. Tidal runs over the site can be strong.

You could hardly say that the Littlehampton Offshore Diving Company, which acts on behalf of many of the dive boats there, tries to keep the wreck to themselves. Most years the site is buoyed by them to assist inflatable cox'ns to find it. Bookings for boats and diving advice from Ray Lee, a diver-skipper himself, at 3, Mayfield, East Preston, West Sussex. Tel: Rustington (0903) 783541.

The marks for inflatable cox'ns to find the *Pine* are as follows: Go to the Winter Buoy, which is on a bearing of 200° from Littlehampton Harbour. Once there turn on to 240°. After less than a mile, look back and you will see two dark round clumps of trees on the shoreline to the left of Littlehampton Harbour. This is Clymping Clump. Now put Littlehampton water tower into the middle of these tree clumps. Continue on that line. Next pick out Bognor water tower and place the left edge on the right-hand edge of Butlins Holiday Camp. You should then be right over the remains of the *Pine*.

Littlehampton has easy launching facilities. There is the public launch site at Fisherman's Quay on the East Bank of the River Arun. A tractor service is available for hauling up and lowering down the steep ramp for a fee. This service is run by Britannia Watersports, the dive shop where Ken Buttle, the owner, will also supply air to 4000 psi. Tel: Littlehampton (0903) 722222. There is also easy launching for a fee at Littlehampton Marina on the West Bank, where "Tish" Neale is the manager. Tel. Littlehampton (0903) 713553. Air is also available.

Those who would like to dive the *Caleb Sprague* will need to charter a boat from Newhaven. The wreck, which is 250-feet long, is upright with her bows to the West at 50 38 15; 00 25 29. Her highest point is her bridge amidships some 11 metres off the 46 metre seabed. There has been some salvage work on her cargo of steel. The torpedo damage is clear on her port side. Her bell has been raised. Diving the *Emerald* will also need a Newhaven boat. She is at 50 38 18; 00 25 35 and shallower than the *Caleb Sprague* at 37 metres. She stands 10 metres proud with a long sandbank rising to the North of the 202-foot-long wreck.

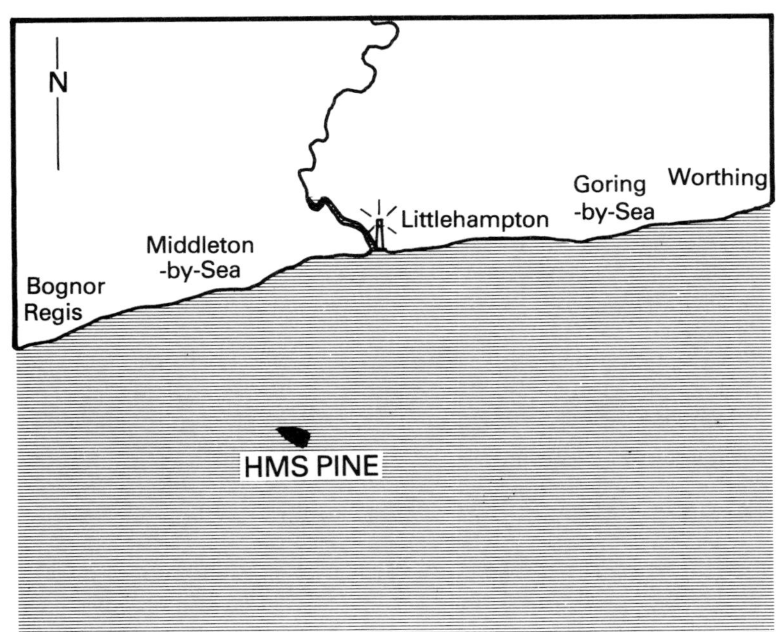

The 'Pine' is well broken, in shallow water.

Pine wreck log

Position: 50 43 05; 00 37 10W.

Littlehampton, Sussex

Chart No.: 1652

Date: ....

Dive leader: ....

Equipment used:
ABLJ/STAB .... Air capacity: ....

Suit .... Demand valve ....

Weights: .... SMB/reel ....

Special equipment ....

Dive Boat: ....

Weather .... Sea Height .... State of tide ....

Current .... Underwater viz ....

Dive timing:
Left surface .... Returned surface ....

Maximum depth: ....

Decompression required ....

Seabed type .... Scour present ....

State of wreckage ....

Area of ship dived: ....

Special points to note: ....

....

Contemporary print of the 'Brazen' wrecking.

CHAPTER SIX

HMS Brazen

HE COULDN'T SWIM and his name was Jeremiah, but he really had nothing to moan about – he was the only survivor of a crew of 105. Not that it was easy to save him. To do so they had to lower a wooden cage into the sea and then crank him and his rescuers 300 feet up the sheer face of the great white cliffs of crumbly chalk near Newhaven, Sussex. The story of Jeremiah Hill is the story of His Majesty's sloop-of-war *Brazen* of 18 guns, commanded by Captain James Hanson, and wrecked in the early hours of January 26, 1800.

There have been ships called *Brazen* in the Navy since the time of Drake. Not great ships of the line, but fast and daring sloops, brigs and destroyers. There's been a *Brazen* in the thick of each and every war which Britain fought at sea. But as the years have gone by the *Brazens* have grown in size. The HMS *Brazen*, for example, which had Prince Andrew as her helicopter pilot was a 4000-ton frigate. That's a big increase on the little *Brazen* of that wreck of 1800. She was only 363 tons. In the days when she was wrecked England was at war with France and good seamen were hard to find.

Early in January, 1800, *Brazen* was waiting at Portsmouth, short-handed. The press gangs were waiting too – for the crews which had been paid off from one ship so that they could crack them back into yet another. Some crews didn't even set foot ashore. They were paid, but were then "drafted" into ships which needed men like HMS *Brazen*. They got Jeremiah Hill that way. He was drafted from the frigate *Carysfort*. Hill was one of the last to come aboard, and on January 16, 1800 the *Brazen* set sail for Channel patrol duties and was sent off towards Newhaven to deal with some "insolent attacks" in that area by marauding French vessels. The *Brazen* was small – 105 feet long with a 28-foot beam – was flush-decked and only 14 feet in depth. This gave little accommodation for the crew who lived in what can only be described as extreme discomfort. To off-set this was the fact that ships like the *Brazen* were fast and free-ranging, and there was always the chance of prize money to be picked up.

Captain Hanson was a good captain, much more experienced than those of the other 103 sloops on the Navy List at that time. He had served from 1791 to 1794 with Captain George Vancouver while they explored Australia, New Zealand and Hawaii. He then stayed with Vancouver while he surveyed the American coast and gave his name to Vancouver Island. Not that Hanson had commanded *Brazen* for long. She was, in fact, a prize herself – the former French privateer *Bonaparte*, captured in April 1799. Whether the crew regarded this as a good or bad omen we do not know. We do know that they ran into bad weather in the Channel. Gales followed one another in seemingly endless succession. So much so that a ship called *Richard Thompson* which set out for Newcastle from London was driven, like the Spanish Armada, round the Orkneys and ended up in Falmouth!

The *Brazen* rode out one near-hurricane, and then in the lull had a bit of good luck. Just off the Isle of Wight she ran down and took a storm-battered French merchantman and sent her back as a prize to Portsmouth under control of the master's mate, a midshipman, eight seamen and two well-armed marines. On

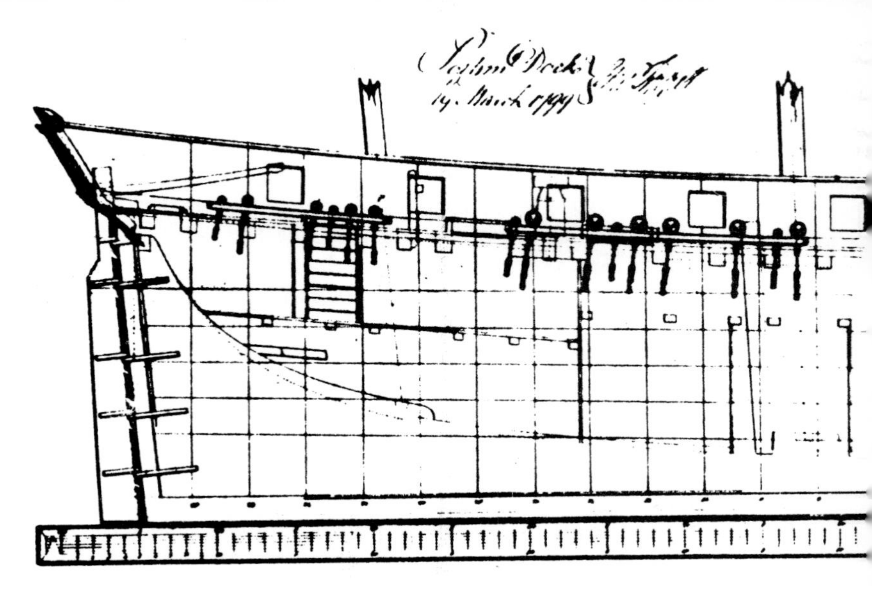

January 25 the ships parted company and the lull was over. In the evening the wind came back stronger than ever, and this time was carrying heavy rain with it. The *Brazen* ran before it. Jeremiah Hill came on watch at 10 pm that Saturday night. During his watch the wind grew to a full gale from the South-West and showed no sign of lessening. Hill was relieved at 2 am, but it is a clear indication of conditions below deck that he did not go down to his hammock until 4 am. At five o'clock in the morning, the crash of her striking had him racing up on deck with jacket and "trowsers" in his hands. He had no time to put either garment on, and within moments was part of a team under John Teague, the ship's carpenter, cutting through the weather shrouds to let the

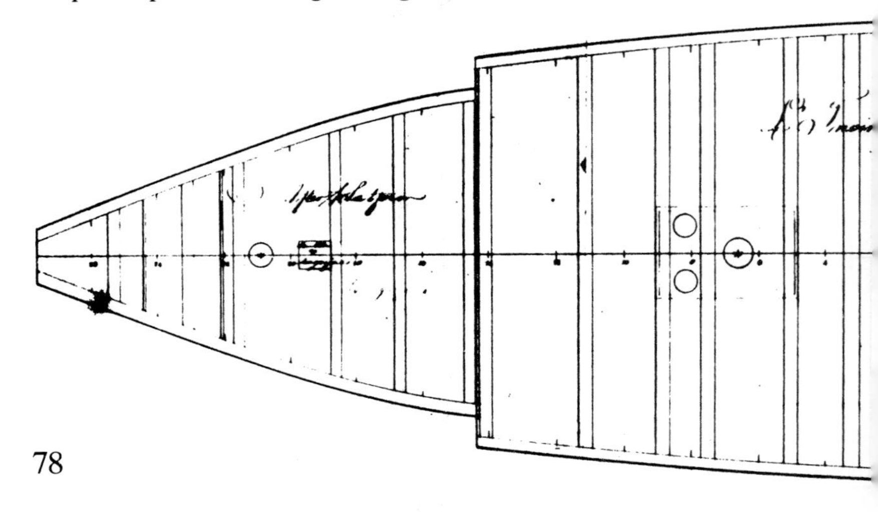

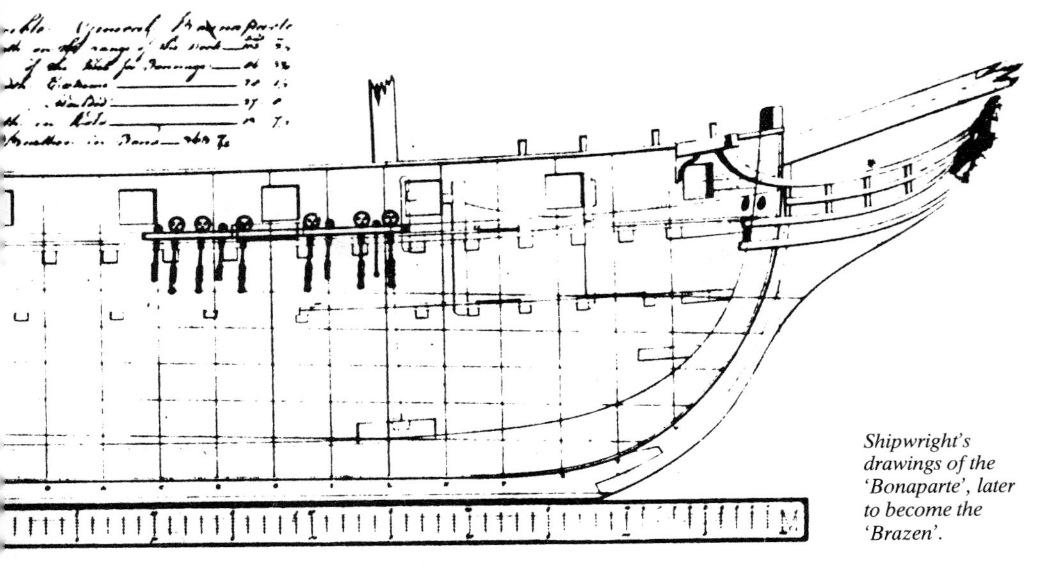

Shipwright's drawings of the 'Bonaparte', later to become the 'Brazen'.

main and mizen masts go by the board. The masts crashed down all right, but it didn't do much good as the ship was soon pushed on to her side by the huge waves which swept over her. This sudden topple is the reason that no signal guns of distress were fired. Jeremiah Hill got to the stump of the mainmast and clung on desperately as the sky lightened a little and the dark shape of the shore cliffs could be made out. It seems certain that it was during this first striking that Captain Hanson was swept overboard and never seen again.

On shore the first report of the wreck sent a horseman thundering off the nine miles to Brighton in search of Captain Sproule of the Royal Navy, who commanded this section of the

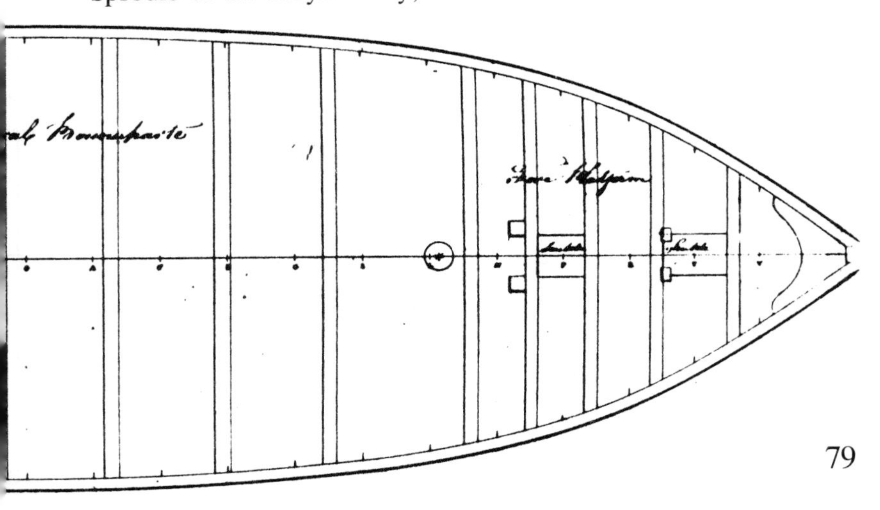

SINGULAR PRESERVATION OF THE ONLY SURVIVOR OF THE WRECK OF THE BRAZEN.

coast. Other people rushed along the shore towards the cries of the stranded men. At daybreak the wreck was seen to be half a mile off. The masts were all gone, but there were parts of the ship which, in between waves, were clear of the water, and on these points survivors could be seen from the shore. There was nothing, though, that those on shore could do. The tide was making and the would-be rescuers on the beach had to retreat round the point of rock to another bay to save being cut off by the waves. As the tide raced in, up on the cliffs two extraordinary machines were pulled by horses close to the edge of the sheer drop. These machines had been made for just this sort of emergency. An arm could be swung out over the edge and from a rope through a pulley-wheel, a big wooden cage could be lowered down to the shore. The cage was big enough to hold three men. Seeing that some of the sailors might still make the shore, two men gallantly let themselves be lowered in the cage to the small area not yet covered by the tide.

On the wreck, seeing these preparations to save them, Lieutenant James Cook and the Purser, John Braugh, both excellent swimmers, stripped off and struck out for land. They nearly made it, but one after the other sank, exhausted. Another near-survivor got so close that the men from the cage were in the surf trying to reach him when a loose piece of sail from the ship was thrown over him by a wave and the bundle was carried out to sea. Jeremiah Hill knew he could not hold on much longer and was thinking of letting go and ending it all when part of the sliding carriage from one of the ship's carronades floated to his hands. It was better than nothing and so he clung to it. The solid block of wood carried him safely to shore, where the two men grabbed him and dragged him to the cage. It was time to go. Within minutes of the three men being drawn up to the cliff-top the waves were breaking fifty feet up the cliffs! It was a long time before Jeremiah Hill was strong enough to speak. It was not until he did so that the rescuers knew the name of his ship.

The wreck broke up quickly. The stern post with two of the guns was washed ashore, some timber was driven right past the Eastern pier of Newhaven harbour entrance before it too came ashore. Someone at the time calculated that the 95 bodies so far washed ashore must have possessed at least £500 in cash and bills – because they had been so recently paid off from other ships. But no more of that was heard. Wagons from Newhaven collected the dead and on the next Saturday afternoon all that were recovered so far were buried "in a spot of ground adjoining the churchyard". (It was not until July 1808 that an Act of Parliament required bodies cast ashore to be given a Christian burial in consecrated ground). A report of the time said: "A handsome stone monument, or pillar, commemorative of the melancholy event, has been erected near the grave which contains their reliques, at the expense of Captain Hanson's family, from a very appropriate design of Mr. Henry Rhodes, architect." It is doubtful though that the grave contains the remains of the Captain.

A letter from Lewes of February 3 that year says: "Captain Hanson's widow, who is far advanced in her pregnancy, has expressed a strong desire to see the remains of her husband; in consequence of which a reward has been offered for the recovery of his body, which is distinguishable by an anchor marked with gunpowder on one of his arms." But despite the reward and the tattoo mark there is no record of his body being recovered and the four plaques on the sides of the memorial, while telling the story of the *Brazen* and listing the officers' names, seem to take care not to go further than saying: "The remains of many of them were interred near to this spot by the direction of the Lords Commissioners of The Admiralty." Louisa, Captain Hanson's widow, didn't die until she was 104 in 1884!

The 'Brazen' under sail off Newhaven.

If they didn't find the Captain's body, they didn't raise her cannon either. There is no record of any salvage of the *Brazen* or her guns – apart from the two washed ashore with part of her stern. This lack of salvage is surprising. It may of course have been done without any written record of it. Or the written record may have been lost. Or the salvage report may be buried in the wrong file in Naval records at the Public Record Office. It may of course show that they couldn't find the wreck when they went to salvage the guns. Certainly, until very recently, divers could not find the wreck or any traces of it. The trouble was that wreck reports of the time used names of rocks and reefs which aren't called that any more. Take the *Monthly Register of Naval Events* for the time. That says: "The *Brazen* sloop of war, mounting 18 guns, commanded by Captain Hanson was, in a gale of wind, driven on Ave Rocks near Newhaven." No one today knows the Ave Rocks. The Hydrographic Department of the Ministry of Defence in Somerset conducted a search through old charts for me and found no Ave Rocks. Mr. Victor H. Bourne of the Newhaven and Seaford Historical Society, which runs a splendid local museum under the cliffs of the West Foreshore (open Good Friday to the end of October), wrote to me to say that they have usually identified the Ave Rocks of the past with the "Fricker, Friggle or Frigger" rocks near Old Nore Point.

Take the *Mariner's Chronicle* of 1810. That says the spot is "about one mile to the westward" of Newhaven. It adds that the wreck was "about half-a-mile from shore". The distance of the Fricker Rocks from Newhaven is certainly not a mile. Take *The Seaman's Recorder* of the time. That tells us that the tide "had flowed so high as to prevent any one from passing round the points of the rocks that projected far into the sea." In other words, we are looking for a bay which is completely cut off by the sea at high tide with reefs which stick well out on either one or both sides of it.

And finally, just to confuse all our research so far, take *The Times* of January 28, 1800. It reported that a letter from Brighton said that the *Brazen* "struck on a reef of rocks at Westmiss Rope, nearly two miles from Newhaven and seven from Brighton". That would contradict all the other reports and put the wreck almost opposite the middle of Peacehaven (which was open downland until 1915). And would you believe it, no one can find any trace of a "Westmiss Rope". Having dug out those conflicting facts, I found myself hooked on the idea of diving the *Brazen* myself. But where was she? I hunted through all the local archives and found nothing more. So I decided to walk the ground and get the whole area into perspective. First I visited the churchyard of one of the oldest Norman churches in England, St. Michael's, the parish church of Newhaven. There is the memorial to the loss of the *Brazen*, which is now included in the graveyard. There are four inscribed slate panels on this big railed-off monument. They read as follows:

No. 1.

SACRED
To the memory
Of
CAPTAIN JAMES HANSON,
The Officers and Company of His Majesty's ship
BRAZEN;
Who was wrecked in a violent storm
Under the cliff,
Bearing from this place, S.W.
At five o'clock A.M. January 26th, 1800;
One of the crew only surviving to tell the melancholy tale.
By this fatal event
The country, alas! was deprived of 105 brave defenders,
At a time when it
Most required their assistance:
The remains of many of them were interred near to this spot,
By the direction of
The Lords Commissioners of the Admiralty.
"The waters saw thee, O God!"

No. 2.

THE BRAZEN
Had been ordered to protect this part of the coast from the insolent attacks of the enemy;
And in the evening preceding the sad catastrophe,
Had detained a foreign vessel,
Which
Was put under the care of the master's mate, a midshipman, eight seamen, and two marines;
Who were thereby saved from the fate of their companions.

No. 3

NAMES OF THE OFFICERS LOST.
James Hanson, Esq. Commander.
James Cook, John Dembry, Lieutenants.
Archibald Ingram, Master.
Patrick Venables, James Hanwell, Midshipmen.
John Braugh, Purser.
Robert Still, Surgeon.
Thomas Whitfield, Boatswain.
Robert Alder Yawrle, Gunner.
John Teague, Carpenter.

No. 4

The friends of
CAPTAIN HANSON
Caused this monument to be erected
As a mark of their esteem for a deserving officer,
And a valuable friend:
It was the will of Heaven
To preserve him
During a four years voyage of danger and difficulty.
Round the world,
On discoveries
With Captain Vancouver,
In the years 1791, 1792, 1793, 1794,
But to take him from us
When he thought himself
Secure.
"The voice of the Lord is upon the waters."

Having made one tour around the four panels, I went back to the first and read it again. And then it hit me. It reads: "Sacred to the memory of Captain James Hanson, the Officers and Company of His Majesty's ship Brazen; Who was wrecked in a violent storm under the cliff bearing from this place SW..." Bearing South-West from this place. It seemed an odd thing to put on a tombstone. Could it be a real bearing? Put there by sea-faring men. It sounded a bit like *Treasure Island* and all that. However, once back home, having bought the Ordnance Survey Sheet TQ 40 SW, which covers the area and is the metric version of the old six-inches-to-the-mile map, I carefully drew a line South-West from the site of the memorial.

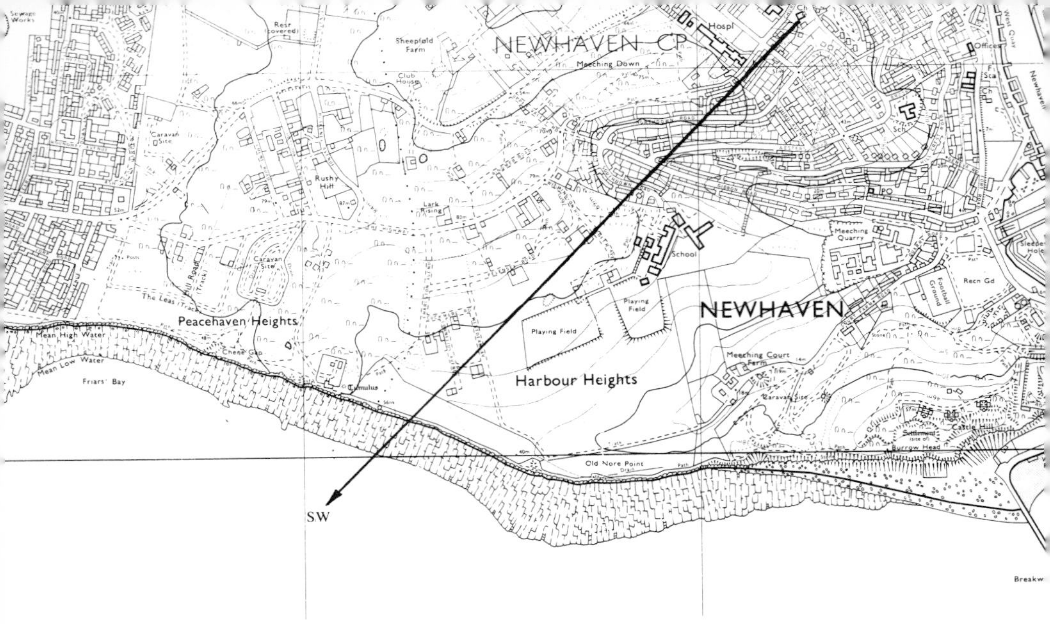

The SW bearing from the 'Brazen' memorial. Bottom: the memorial.

The fact that the line bisects the cliff almost exactly a mile to the West of Newhaven made me certain that the bearing is a true one. Once again I walked the ground and right into a South-Westerly gale which violently confirmed my admiration for those who in similar January conditions had swayed and bumped down the cliff and up again in the primitive cage 184 years ago to rescue Jeremiah Hill. Despite the battering of the wind, I found my bearing cuts the cliff top line just to the east of the Ministry of Defence's rusting old Nissen huts in a high-fenced perimeter on the top of the cliffs. This is an easy mark to spot from the sea. Mind you, I had not allowed for magnetic variations in my bearing and no doubt someone could come up with a more accurate fix for the 1800's. As far as I could see without being blown over the edge, the spot below my mark fitted all the facts.

Diving the Brazen

SHORTLY AFTER PUBLISHING these details of my search in *Diver* magazine, I was delighted to hear from several divers that they had found traces of an old Naval wreck not so far from my bearing. Their discoveries were made on and close to the West of the Fricker, Friggle or Frigger Rocks (you will find all spellings on old maps and charts). The area is heavily silted and visibility was usually poor, but discoveries so far include a short bronze pin bearing the Admiralty's broad arrow mark, a sword blade, a five-foot long anchor, a 20-foot section of something very like a mast, together with massive timbers 17 ft by 2 ft, and a cast-iron swivel gun. Divers should report any finds to Peter Bailey, the Curator of Newhaven Museum Tel: Newhaven (0273) 514760, who is a great enthusiast about the *Brazen*. The bronze pin is on display in the museum, which has a great deal of other wreck material.

The Fricker Rocks lie just off Old Nore Point, which is the first point to the West of Newhaven Harbour Breakwater at 50 46 36; 00 02 15E. Depths run up to 10 metres and the rocks are spread over a wide area. Divers should be warned that nets for sole and plaice have been reported as being laid close to this area.

Newhaven Harbour is on the River Ouse and an 8-knot speed limit is always in operation. The harbour is *not* well served by public launch sites suitable for inflatables and other small boats. But there is one site between Quay 10 and Quay 11 on the road called Riverside which runs along West Quay. It is only suitable for use at or near High Water. If you launch here, the harbour-master, Captain Alec Flint, advises care when threading your way through the numerous trawler moorings.

Another do-it-yourself launching ramp lies at Meeching Boats, Denton Island. This is further up-river, but a concrete ramp allows launching from half-tide. A year's rent of a key which will open the padlock on the chain which bars access to the ramp, will cost about £27 for a 14ft boat and not much more for anything bigger. Write to Meeching boats or ring Newhaven (0273) 514907 for further details. You can leave your boat there overnight for no extra charge.

If you like the easy life, Newhaven Marina Limited will launch and recover boats daily in the marina, which is on the West side of

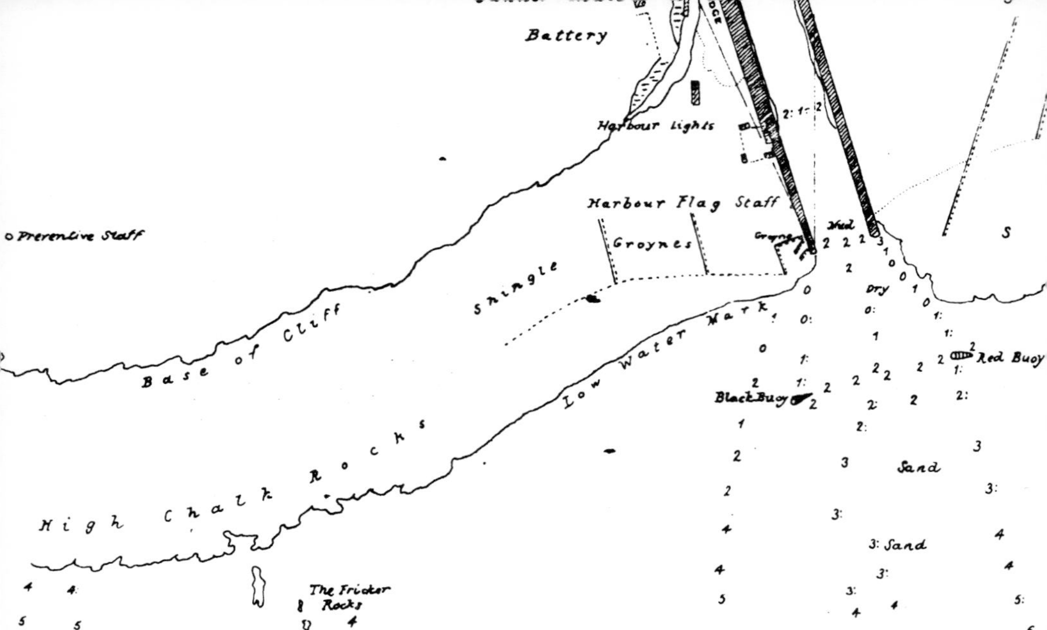

Location of Fricker Rocks on a Victorian map.

the river nearer to the mouth. Boats up to 20ft are charged about £10 on a weekday for this service, and £15 at weekends and Bank Holidays. Overnight moorings for your boat, by prior arrangement, are about £5 per night. Divers using the marina facilities should ask at the office and will be given access to hot showers and toilets free of charge. Late-rising divers should, however, be warned that in times of exceptional demand such as hot sunny weekends and Bank Holidays, with the marina's two tractors launching boat after boat for hours in the morning, late-comers may be turned away for the simple reason that the marina know that all the boats launched earlier will have to be taken out and any more would involve their working all night! The marina tell me that it happens only rarely, but it *does* happen. There is no booking system for launching. It is first come, first served.

Divers using the harbour should take care, as the heavy traffic includes the Sealink ferry service to Dieppe. There are traffic signals at the entrance to the harbour on the Southern end of West Pier, where the harbour control is situated. Signals used during daytime are –

Entry permitted: Red triangle over red ball.
Departure permitted: Red ball over red triangle.
Free to move in or out: Red ball.
No movement permitted: Red ball over red triangle over red ball.

HMS BRAZEN

The river is silting, and dredging takes place almost continuously. The silt is dredged away, too, from the mouth of the river so there is no real bar there now. The shallowest depth of 4.5 metres, where the silt does try to form a bar at the end of the breakwater can, however, produce a short, sharp sea.

Boat launching at Seaford can be undertaken almost anywhere over the steep shingle beach. There is no proper launching ramp, and all boats have to be carried down from the seawall and heaved across the beach. This is all very well on the way down, but the return journey can be exhausting. Fortunately, car-parking is easy on the roadway at the back of the wall. There is a toilet block near the Martello Tower.

Air is available from the C and E Sports Centre, 15, Bridge Street, Newhaven. Tel: Newhaven (0273) 515450. This is a sports shop retailing diving equipment. They pump to 3000 psi. Open 9 am to 6 pm, except Wednesdays and Sundays, when hours are 9 am to 1 pm. Hard boats can be arranged through the marina. Tel: Newhaven (0273) 513881.

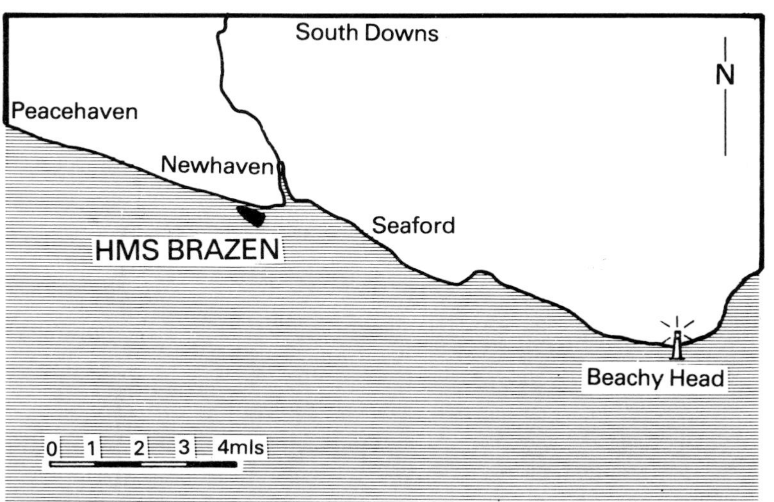

The 'Brazen' lies to the West of the Fricker Rocks.

Brazen wreck log

Position: 50 46 36; 00 02 15E.

Fricker Rocks, Newhaven, Sussex

Chart No.: 1652

Date: ....

Dive leader: ....

Equipment used:
ABLJ/STAB .... Air capacity: ....

Suit .... Demand valve ....

Weights: .... SMB/reel ....

Special equipment ....

Dive Boat: ....

Weather .... Sea Height .... State of tide ....

Current .... Underwater viz ....

Dive timing:
Left surface .... Returned surface ....

Maximum depth: ....

Decompression required ....

Seabed type .... Scour present ....

State of wreckage ....

Area of ship dived: ....

Special points to note: ....

....

CHAPTER SEVEN

The Andola

A SAILOR'S LIFE was a hard one. But it wasn't half as hard as the hearts of some Victorian shipowners. There was no limit to the voyages on which they would send their ships in search of profit. If there was money to be made by sending coke to Mexico, they sent it. If there was more to be made by sending that same ship without a break another 2000 miles to pick up a cargo of wheat for a homeward voyage, they sent it. All those Victorian sayings so beloved of the businessman – "Time is money", "Where there's muck there's brass" – were, it seemed, never far from the lips of those who owned ships in those hard times. The stories of their callousness are legion, but few tales of shipwreck illustrate the testing life of a Victorian seaman, and condemn those who ordered him from port to port, better than the tale of the last voyage of the three-masted steel-hulled barque they called *Andola*.

Built in Liverpool, the 2093-ton sailing ship was registered there, and Roberts and Company, of the same port, owned her. From Liverpool they sent her in September, 1893, to Barry in Wales for a load of coke. On the seventh of the same month the 275 feet of her hull set sail fully-laden for Santa Rosalia, the Mexican port in the Sea of Cortez, better known as the Gulf of California. It took her nearly six months to make the trip and deliver coke for use in the Baja California copper mines. And then, it seems, her owners couldn't find a cargo for her. Captain Passmore and his crew kicked their heels in Santa Rosalia for two months until they received fresh orders.

Not that her owners didn't try to find a use for her. An idle ship was not something to be allowed. Men could not be paid for doing nothing, sitting about in the sun. Part of the time was taken up taking in tons of stone as ballast, but that was hardly gainful employment. It merely meant that when fresh orders did arrive no time had to be wasted ballasting her. And this time her orders sent her on a 2000-mile run up the Pacific coast of America to

Vancouver Island, followed by a turn in through the Juan de Fuca Strait to Puget Sound and into the port of Seattle. Here *Andola* loaded 2000 tons of wheat before casting off for Falmouth in August, 1894. Captain Passmore – and the owners – expected that voyage to take four months. But then they did not allow for the weather turning as foul as it did. *Andola* ran into gale after gale. No wind, it seemed, was going her way and she was battered endlessly by winds of such force that at one time she was under bare poles for three days. Rounding the Horn nearly finished her, and she was almost swamped on more than one day. At the height of one gale, a huge wave swept right over her, carrying away the ship's boat and smashing everything in its path. Captain Passmore asked for volunteers to clear the wreckage. Four men offered to do the job.

They had no sooner started on the work than another great wave smashed three of them along the deck, injuring them all. The fourth man was lifted straight out of the ship and was never seen again. For the whole of those days the crew lived in sodden clothes, and there was no dry spot for them even in their bunks. The crew began to believe that dreadful voyage would never end. But it did, when, on January 29, 1895, after 180 days at sea and two months overdue, the *Andola* finally entered Falmouth.

If her owners were relieved they showed no sign of it. There was to be no rest for the crew, even after 180 days at sea. Giving them only long enough to take on fresh water and food, the owners ordered the ship to Hull – at once. Hull was where the profit was, and that was where the *Andola* was to discharge her cargo. The ship's brief stop in Falmouth – she came in in the morning and went out on the evening tide – had brought little change in the weather. No sooner had the *Andola* cleared the port and started up Channel than the wind swung right against her. The *Andola* started tacking once again. It seemed to the hands that they had done nothing else for all of their lives. And they were still in the same gear that they had worn right across the Atlantic. The tugs which had brought out the fresh water and food had brought no extra clothing with them.

The tacks of the *Andola* grew larger and larger as she fought to gain ground. So big in fact that she was crossing the entire Channel from side to side. On one leg they could see the lights of France. On the next, the Lizard light lay close. It was then that the crew realised that they were going backwards. To add to their misery, it started to snow, and soon they saw nothing but cold and darkness all around. The deck apprentice, young Alfred Hunt, was certainly serving a full apprenticeship. It was his sharp ears that heard the mournful tolling of the Manacle Buoy. Captain Passmore knew he was too close, and tried to stay his ship, but it was no use. A few minutes later she struck.

Though the Captain and crew could see nothing in the darkness, they had, in fact, struck Shark's Fin Rock, a well-named, thin but tall, slate outcrop, which makes up the outer part of Manacle Point itself. Though they could not see it, they were within a few hundred yards of the Porthoustock Lifeboathouse, whose crew even now were hurrying to launch their boat under the command of Cox'n Tripp. The *Andola's*

The 'Andola' fast on Shark's Fin Rock.

striking had been seen by a duty coastguard on Manacle Point. Captain Passmore hastened to get off distress signals. But the flares only fizzled, probably as a result of the battering and constant dampness of *Andola's* six month voyage.

It seemed that there was nothing that could go wrong which didn't. And to cap it all, when young Alfred Hunt was ordered to fetch some bomb rockets, a kind of maroon, from the stores, he managed to drop the still spluttering flare which he carried into the locker where the rockets were stored. As the flare fell down it burst into full light and Hunt, in a panic, slammed the lid on it and fled up on deck. He wasn't quite quick enough. One of the rockets exploded and buried shrapnel deep in his thigh. Other

rockets went beserk and set fire to the charthouse, injuring the helmsman. Another explosion sent an able seaman crashing to the deck. The noise of the rocket bombs was so loud that they were heard in Falmouth and the Falmouth lifeboat was launched. But nothing could beat the Porthoustock boat to the wreck. She was there within minutes and easily rescued all 28 of the crew.

Now the *Andola* swung beam on to the cliffs under the pounding of sea and wind, but (even though she was soon auctioned for several hundred pounds) there was never any real chance of getting her off. She was holed badly, and soon her cargo of wheat swelled with the water and her plates started in several places. More gales in early February completed the damage, and soon the ship was battered down to the bottom of Porthoustock Bay. She showed for some time, but then one day even at low tide there was nothing to be seen above surface of this victim of a Victorian shipowner's greed.

Diving the Andola

SHE'S NOT DEEP, but she is interesting. She's an ideal dive for a beginner or an amusing one for a second dive after a deep one on the Manacles nearby. Her wreckage is at 50 03 18; 05 03 30. Best time to dive her is in the Spring before the heavy weed of Summer cloaks her tightly, but as the weed even then is not that tall you'll find no difficulty in moving over her at any time. Maximum depth is 10 metres. The lazy can locate her from a boat, but my first dive on her was done by carrying the gear to the sandy strip just opposite her below the Point, and then she's so close – about 40 yards – that we didn't even bother to go out on snorkel.

You can't miss Shark's Fin Rock, and *Andola* is inside the rock to the North and in towards the beach at Porthoustock. Her bow is to the South and broken plates and ribs are all around. Some sections of her double bottom can still be clearly seen. Near the bow are great lengths of her anchor chain. It is around the bow that the "treasure" of the *Andola* lies. You see she carried her name on both sides of her bow in brass letters nearly a foot high, each of which weighed close to four pounds. Some of those letters

THE ANDOLA

have been recovered, but others may remain there still.

If you want to dive her by boat then launch off the close-by Porthoustock beach, where there are toilets and a cafe. Keep well clear of the left-hand side of the beach, where there are fishing boats and winches to pull them up. St. Keverne is the nearest large village to the site, and there is plenty of bed-and-breakfast accommodation in the area. Air is often available from a compressor on Porthkerris Beach – the next bay round to the North of Porthoustock – otherwise the nearest source is the holiday camp at Mullion where they will pump to 3,500 psi.

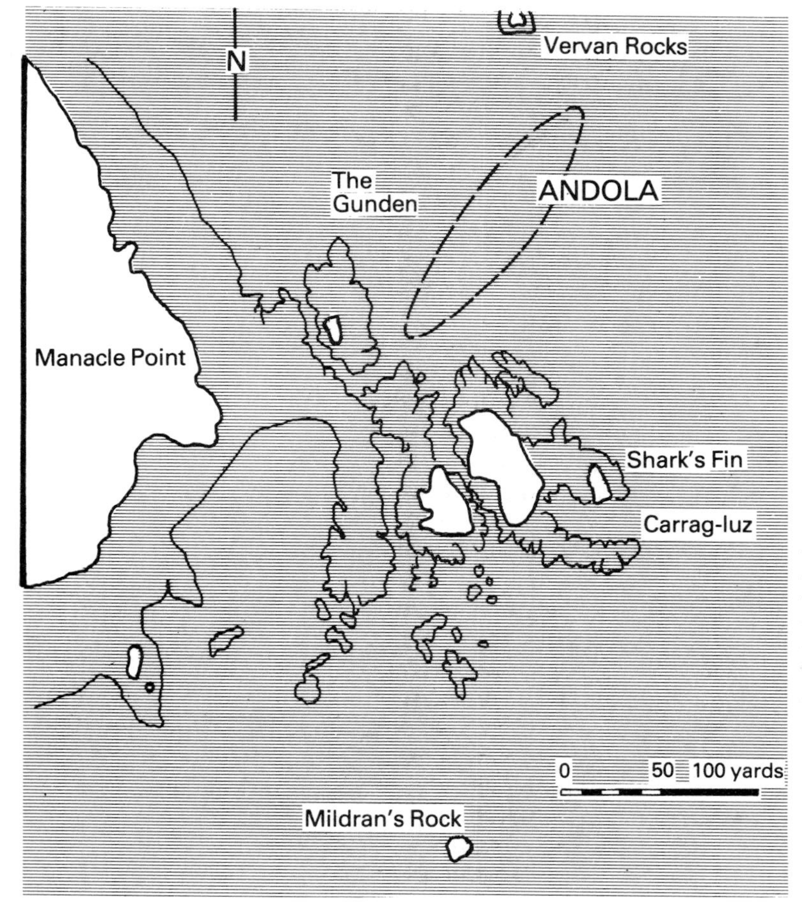

The 'Andola' is at a depth of 10 metres, 40 yards out from the beach at Porthoustock.

Andola wreck log

Position: 50 03 18; 05 03 30W.

Shark's Fin Rock, Porthoustock, Cornwall

Chart No.: 777

Date: ....

Dive leader: ....

Equipment used:
ABLJ/STAB .... Air capacity: ....

Suit.. Demand valve ....

Weights: .... SMB/reel ....

Special equipment ....

Dive Boat: ....

Weather..........................Sea Height...........State of tide...........

Current ....Underwater viz ....

Dive timing:
Left surface ....Returned surface..........................

Maximum depth:...

Decompression required..

Seabed type.............................Scour present ....

State of wreckage ....

Area of ship dived: ....

Special points to note: ....

....

CHAPTER EIGHT

The UB-81

A GREAT GREY GHOST from the past, crewed by dead men, she moved over the seabed of the Channel miles away from the place in which she was sunk. In her tanks there was still just enough air left to hold her up off the seabed and let her ride the tide for nearly 70 years. Inside her rusting hull were 26 crew and their much decorated commander, who had come so very close to saving them all. In her travels that German submarine, *UB-81*, had covered miles and miles, but now lies, stopped, it seems for ever, over 20 miles in a direct line from the site of her sinking in 1917. She has been found by divers twice in recent years in very different positions. She is now shattered at bow as well as stern, and there is no lift left in her. It looks as though she has come to her final resting place, though you never know – she has moved over five miles in the past 15 years.

The *UB-81* never completed her first mission, which was also

her last. It was either sheer bad luck which sank her or very skilful mine laying by the Royal Navy, depending on which side you were on. Certainly it was no fault of her captain, Reinhold Salzwedel, who was one of the most experienced and aggressive commanders of the Flanders Flotilla. He was said to be "the fair-haired boy of the Flanders base" ... "An upstanding chap, blond and blue-eyed with a fine wide brow, a firm chin, a humorous mouth, and a proud carriage of head – a gallant, laughing, frank-eyed boy, as far as possible from the popular conception of the barbarous Hun." Well, that's as may be, but he certainly was a very successful submarine commander. He ranked 11th in the table of record sinkings of all U-boat captains, having sunk 150,000 tons of Allied shipping on 12 missions from Zeebrugge. He commanded *UB-10*, *UC-21* and *UC-71*, before taking out *UB-81* on her maiden voyage. He had been decorated many times, and was the holder of the coveted "Blue Max", the Pour le Mérite cross, Germany's highest honour of World War One.

This award was given to him after his action against the Q-ship HMS *Dunraven*, commanded by a man who held Britain's highest war decoration, the Victoria Cross, Captain Gordon Campbell. It was August 8, 1917, when Salzwedel in *UC-71* spotted the *Dunraven* zigzagging along in the Bay of Biscay. At first sight she appeared to be an innocent British steamer, armed with only a

U-boat of the UB–81's class.

small gun on her stern. The gun was little threat and in keeping with her status, as most British merchant ships were armed by this stage in the war. Though Salzwedel spotted the *Dunraven* through his six-foot high periscope at 11 o'clock in the morning, he did not know that the hidden Royal Navy crew of the Q-ship were already at action stations behind their concealed guns, having spotted him some minutes earlier. But Salzwedel was no easy meat. He knew all about Q-ships, and didn't exactly like the look of the *Dunraven*. However, after a long and careful inspection, he obviously decided the steamer was all that she seemed to be, and he surfaced 5,000 yards off her starboard bow and opened fire with his 8.8 cm gun.

The *Dunraven* returned the fire with her stern gun, and at the same time reduced speed to let Salzwedel catch up with her. Wireless signals were transmitted for the benefit of the radio man on *UC-71* – "Help! Come quickly! Being chased and shelled by submarine ..." And when *UC-71's* shells started falling close, the *Dunraven* stopped and a "panic party" played the role of the crew abandoning ship. The *Dunraven* was now hit by German shells and set on fire aft. Despite the fact that he knew that the after-magazine must explode if he waited and that a gun and gun crew were concealed over it, Captain Campbell hung on, hoping to get the submarine in really close. A moment later there was a huge explosion aft and the four-inch gun hidden there and the gun crew were all hurled up in the air.

To say this blew the ship's cover is an understatment! Salzwedel knew now what kind of ship he was fighting, and crash-dived. While he did so the aft gun crew were all recovered from the sea and other parts of the ship in which they had landed, and though some were seriously injured, none were killed. Now the *Dunraven* was unmasked, her White Ensign was flown, and her guns unveiled. Another "panic party" left as the ship blazed, but Campbell and a small team remained hidden, hoping that the submarine would surface once again. They knew that a torpedo would be the next logical thing for Salzwedel to employ against them – and he did. The torpedo struck the Q-ship amidships and nearly broke the *Dunraven* in half. And still Campbell and his men lay hidden. The deck beneath them was now getting red-hot, and the British sailors held the boxes of cordite off the decks in their hands to keep them from exploding.

Salzwedel now showed his experience and skill. He rose to the surface exactly astern, where no gun could train on him, and shelled the ship for 20 minutes. Then he submerged again and steamed around her examining her carefully through his periscope. And then Campbell played his last card. He still had two torpedoes and he fired these one after the other at *UC-71*. Both missed, and Salzwedel swiftly submerged. Campbell waited then for another torpedo to strike *Dunraven*, but it never came. Salzwedel had used up his last torpedo. Later, the *Dunraven* capsized and sank. And Salzwedel returned home a hero. Not only had he sunk a Q-ship, but he had also defeated Captain Gordon Campbell, who had already sent *U-68*, *UC-29* and *U-83*, to the bottom. Salzwedel's account of the action against the *Dunraven* confirmed that he had heard the second torpedo go past his conning tower, but had no torpedos left with which to finish off the ship.

Capt Gordon Campbell.

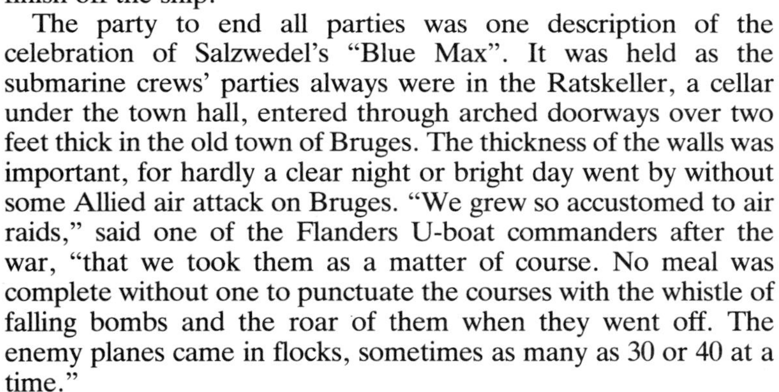

The party to end all parties was one description of the celebration of Salzwedel's "Blue Max". It was held as the submarine crews' parties always were in the Ratskeller, a cellar under the town hall, entered through arched doorways over two feet thick in the old town of Bruges. The thickness of the walls was important, for hardly a clear night or bright day went by without some Allied air attack on Bruges. "We grew so accustomed to air raids," said one of the Flanders U-boat commanders after the war, "that we took them as a matter of course. No meal was complete without one to punctuate the courses with the whistle of falling bombs and the roar of them when they went off. The enemy planes came in flocks, sometimes as many as 30 or 40 at a time."

But they seldom hit their targets – the U-boats. These were kept in "stables" with as many as 25 side by side, under cover of a roof of cement, iron and gravel more than six feet thick, which the bombs could not penetrate. It was a different matter in the streets. All over Bruges buildings were wrecked and craters torn in the roads. So when the U-boat men held their nightly parties, they chose somewhere where no bomb was likely to penetrate. And that place most nights was the Ratskeller. The noise inside would have done credit to any modern disco. And the decoration matched the U-boat men's tomorrow-we-die mood. One huge mural in the cellar showed John Bull as the figurehead of a British ship which was being towed into Zeebrugge by a group of U-boats. On the opposite wall was a mural of a card game with a difference. The players were mines and the stakes German submarines.

Overleaf: Dramatic photograph of the 'Dunraven' sinking, taken from the deck by a crew member.

But there was to be no partying in the Ratskeller for Salzwedel and his crew in the evening of November 28, 1917. All the previous week they had been working up their new boat, the *UB-81*. She was brand-new, 650 tons, with four bow and one stern torpedo tubes. She carried 10 50-cm torpedoes, and had completed her sea trials with flying colours. On the surface her top speed was 13.4 knots, submerged she could make nearly eight. But most important to the crew was the fact that she could get under completely in a crash dive in less than 30 seconds. They liked that and felt they had a good boat as well as a good captain. No one however noticed that *UB-81's* first mission was to be Salzwedel's 13th.

The start of unlucky 13 for Salzwedel began in that late evening of November 28, as he conned the 182-foot-long submarine down the canal from the Bruges submarine pens to the sea at Zeebrugge. Once out in the open, a careful course was set on the surface to avoid the British minefields before diving to the seabed and running the gauntlet of the mines and nets of the Dover Barrage, which stretched from French coast to British beach and had already killed ten U-boats. But *UB-81* was lucky this time for she got through the Folkestone end of the Barrage without being detected. Salzwedel wasted no time, and before midnight on November 30 he was in action attacking a convoy, "approximately 12 sea miles West of Beachy Head". But he had no success.

The next day he was further down Channel, where he sank "the armed English steamer *Molesan*" with a single torpedo. He got the name slightly wrong. The ship he sank was the armed merchantman *Molesey* of 3218 tons. Though the *Molesey* was torpedoed without warning, she did stay afloat long enough for the crew to take to the boats. The *Molesey* sank down to the seabed at 50 35 23; 00 27 24, where today she is badly rusted and in 45m of water. Divers who have visited her say that she is almost completely upside down, and that the hull has rusted right through in many places. Her iron propellor is still in place, and she stands some six metres proud of the seabed ridge on which she lies.

Salzwedel, like many other U-boat commanders, found the area around lightships a particularly good hunting ground. So, the day after he sank the *Molesey*, and after attacking another British ship which avoided his torpedo and scurried safely away in a westerly direction, he set course westward too – for the Owers Lightship. And as the weather had become very stormy and the ride on the surface thoroughly uncomfortable for all 34 on board, Salzwedel took the *UB-81* down to 20m for a smoother run. At 5.45 pm on December 2, when the U-boat was two nautical miles South of the Owers Lightship, a tremendous explosion threw her sideways. Lights went out and water spurted into the stern compartment. She sank swiftly downwards and settled heavily on the seabed at 30m. With the added depth the inflow of water increased rapidly, and the only thing to do was to slam the watertight hatch and seal off the rear compartment entirely. But despite the battering the explosion had given the boat, not one of the crew was injured. And a swift check of the rest of the submarine showed that apart from the stern, she was undamaged.

What Salzwedel hit must have been a British mine, for the Navy was now well aware of the fondness of German U-boat commanders for the area around lightships, and laid fields accordingly. However, it might have been a German mine laid by another U-boat of the UC class from the Zeebrugge base. It made no difference whose mine had done the damage, for no matter how hard Salzwedel and his engineers tried there seemed no way that *UB-81* would surface.

The water in the flooded stern compartment was pinning her down to the seabed. Finally Salzwedel knew that he could not waste any more precious compressed air in trying to get some buoyancy into his stern tanks. It was clear that the explosion had ruptured them. The boat was lost, so now Salzwedel tried to save his crew.

By pumping all his remaining air into the bow tanks, he hoped that he could raise the bow high enough to get the seaward ends of the bow torpedo tubes out of the water and then at least the slimmer members of the crew could get out. All torpedoes were manhandled down to the stern. Torpedoes from loaded bow tubes were withdrawn awkwardly for the boat's bows were already lifting as the air hissed into the forward tanks. Then most of the crew was ordered as far aft as possible. Finally the bow would rise no more. Cautiously, the inside end of the highest bow tube opened. Cold night air rushed into the sub. They had done it! The first man out of the polished tube was Engineer Denker, and he saw how close they had been and still were to disaster. The mouth of the tube was a bare 18 inches above the sea surface, and every moment a wave threatened to break right into it. Quickly, Denker reached down and hoisted Leutnant Freudendahl up on to the slippery slope of the sub's bow. Freudendahl was Salzwedel's second-in-command and as such was to be in charge of the party on the exterior of the submarine. One by one crew members were hauled up – from two tubes now – until there were seven men on the outside and Freudendahl called a halt fearing that any more weight would push the mouth of the tubes under the sea.

The sea was getting up again and each swell seemed to hover over the tube openings on each side though the rest of the bow stopped the sea from plunging straight in. It was icy cold out on the casing, and there was no sign of a ship. All was dark, except for the warning flashes from the lightship. On Salzwedel's orders flare pistols loaded with star shells were discharged into the air and SOS signals flashed by means of a lamp handed up through one of the tubes. But nothing happened, and the men crouched in the cold for hours while their crewmates remained motionless in the stern, straining their ears to catch any of the muffled exchanges between Salzwedel and Freudendahl. Suddenly there was a shout from outside. No one needed telling that an English ship had found them; the noise of engines drummed through the hull. English voices shouted across the water. More engine noises came close as more boats arrived. Outside Freudendahl saw his men transferred to the first English Naval patrol boat to find them. He was last across but before he left he could hear the *UB-81* crew queueing to come up.

He was just speculating about the difficulty which some of the fatter, larger crew members were going to have in the narrow torpedo tubes and wondering whether it would be possible to get them out through the conning tower hatch, which was now not all that far under, when, to his horror, the question became superfluous. One of the British patrol boats, trying to get in close to the stricken sub, was suddenly hurled forward by an exceptionally large wave. The patrol boat's bow bit deep into the U-boat's hull. The screaming hiss of compressed air escaping told it all. Within seconds *UB-81* was gone in a swirl of black water. A moment later great gouts of air burst through the surface in two places from the open torpedo tubes and then there were only the waves hurrying along in the searchlights' beams. There were no more survivors, and it seems likely that Reinhold Salzwedel, the other young lieutenant aboard, and 25 crewmen died very quickly as they would hardly have had the time or the strength to shut the bow tube doors against the December sea.

Diving the UB-81

HOW LONG THE *UB-81* lay where she sank no one can know. It is probable that she got on the move almost at once. Certainly, when the Navy had a look for her in 1961, she was gone – the Navy could get no contact in the area of her sinking, which was almost exactly two miles South of the position of the old Owers Lightship. Then in 1970 she was discovered at 50 27 00; 00 51 00. She was now 12 miles away from the place she sank. In 1974, she was discovered upright on a flat sand and shingle seabed some 14 miles South-East of the Isle of Wight. The diver who found her while working for a salvage firm noted that the only real damage – and that looked slight – appeared to be to her bow, which must be where the British patrol boat sliced into her buoyancy tank. And if the stern looked undamaged, the mine explosion earlier must have ruptured her stern tanks internally.

Today she hasn't moved. Or not much. She is at 50 29 22; 00 58 12, standing five metres high on the seabed 28 metres down. She is upright and lies East-West. To dive her, you will need to hire a big boat out of Littlehampton as she is some 15 miles South-West of Selsey Bill. Or at least she was the last time they dived her!

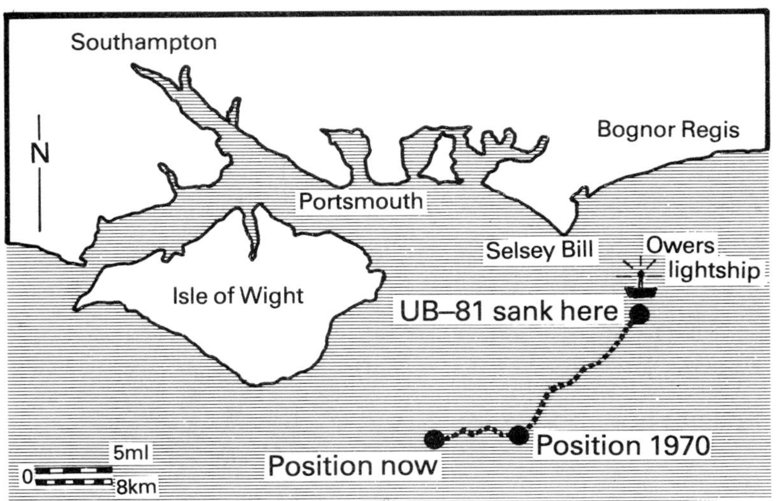

The UB–81 lies in 28 metres of water, 15 miles SW of Selsey Bill.

UB-81 wreck log

Position: 50 29 22; 00 58 12W.

Off Isle of Wight, Hants.

Chart No.: 2045

Date: ....

Dive leader: ....

Equipment used:
ABLJ/STAB .... Air capacity: ....

Suit... Demand valve ....

Weights: .... SMB/reel ....

Special equipment ....

Dive Boat:...

Weather...........................Sea Height...........State of tide...........

Current ....Underwater viz ....

Dive timing:
Left surface ....Returned surface...........................

Maximum depth:...

Decompression required..

Seabed type.............................Scour present ....

State of wreckage ....

Area of ship dived: ....

Special points to note: ....

....

....

....

....

....

....

....

....

....

....

CHAPTER NINE

HMS Weazle

SATURDAY WAS A LOVELY day, crisp and sunny, with no sign of the killer wind which was building up its strength out over the Atlantic. Everybody said how mild it was for February, and what a good day for the party. And so it was, though it was to be the very last party of all for the 106 men and one woman who were to set sail in HMS *Weazle* the next day. But no thought of doom was present at the Saturday night party on board the *Weazle* on February 9, 1799. It was a farewell party, because the *Weazle* was due to sail the next day. And it was a good party. So good, in fact, that many of the inhabitants of Appledore vowed it the best party they had attended in the whole of their lives. Certainly, the Honorable Henry Grey, fourth son of the Earl of Stamford and Warrington, commander of the brig HMS *Weazle*, made sure that all his guests enjoyed themselves. There was no shortage of liquor, some of it confiscated contraband of high quality. For HMS *Weazle* was a brig-of-war engaged in putting down the West Country smuggling traffic, which was in a state of boom at the end of the 18th century.

It is difficult to know just how effective *Weazle* had been, for her crew were very popular. So were the smugglers and their cheap goods. So it is possible to image that the popularity of the men of the *Weazle* was a sign of a not very successful campaign against "the gentlemen". *Weazle* had used Appledore as her home port for a long time, so that by the night of Captain Grey's party the locals knew them all very well. Now the time had come to part. *Weazle* was ordered to Falmouth and after that only the Lords of the Admiralty knew where they would be sent. Most of the crew at the party were sad to be leaving. Falmouth discipline was bound to be tougher than that they had been under in Appledore. Not all of the crew were at the party of course. Some were saying goodbye in other ways in darkened rooms in the town. And some would be glad to go before Summer showed the fruits of Winter sowing.

Appledore is about two-and-a-half miles north of Bideford, North Devon, at the junction of the Torridge and Taw estuaries, and Captain Grey knew that the large sandbanks would mean that he would have to wait for high tide the next afternoon to take *Weazle* out to sea. On that Sunday afternoon a large crowd gathered to wave farewell, and as the tide filled the estuary, the *Weazle's* boats pulled her gently away from the quay. Once well out in mid-stream, the boats were shipped, sails fluttered from the yards and then filled and took her out to sea. One or two women wept, but soon the ship was indistinct in the gathering gloom. Not all of the darkness was due to the fall of evening. There were storms about. However, *Weazle* went safely out through the Neck and over the dangerous Barnstaple Bar. Then she turned her port side towards land and headed west towards Hartland Point. We don't know exactly where she was when the storm broke, but she must have been somewhere between Hartland Point and Lundy Island on her way to Falmouth. We know what time it was when the great North-North-West gale came up – somewhere close to 6 pm because John James of Bideford on February 17, 1799, wrote this in a letter to a friend: "She was in the bay that afternoon, and as the people went to church, the seafaring men felt some anxiety, if the wind should shift a point and blow, which it did".

Captain Grey was now in deep trouble, embayed between Lundy Island and the sheer cliffs of Baggy Point to the north of Appledore. Just what desperate manœuvres he tried, what tacking and running, are all covered by the dark, but slowly he was forced to the North, and all the time was driven closer and closer in to the shore. Just before midnight, the *Weazle* fired her guns as a signal of distress, but there was nothing anyone who heard them could do to help. The distress guns went on at intervals until one in the morning. And then suddenly ceased. The *Weazle* had ploughed into the rocks of Baggy Point and the rest was silence. Writing to report the wreck, Philip Rogers Webber, Lord of the Manor of Croyde noted: "On the tenth instant off Morte Bay Guns of distress was heard from a ship which ceased at one o'clock. At five in the morning a wreck was discovered on the Sands which proved to be His Majesty's Ship Weazel. Great part of her upperworks and Boats all to pieces".

The sands he refers to are the popular surfing beaches of today's Croyde Bay which are backed by high sandhills. And we know from that other letter of the time, from John James, that

Overleaf: how the 'Weazle' was constructed: a contemporary model of her sister ship the 'Alert'.

after the wreck they were lined with people "That fine ship perished and as yet only one body has been taken up, but many are watching from opposite the beach, both yesterday and today, and are fishing up fragments of the wreck. We have since heard that the wreck is visible at low water, this side of Baggy Point".

Not all the crew of the *Weazle* died. In fact one man missed the ship's sailing, and it is tempting to think that he had such a good farewell party that he only awoke after the ship had sailed. Or maybe he stayed too long a-bed in some Appledore lady's arms. The ship's purser, Simon Haly, too, was not on board. He was ashore sick. Letters telling us this can still be seen today in the Public Record Office, though, sadly, they do not mention the reason for the seaman missing the ship. It is interesting to note too that in those same records two of the seamen lost are marked as having joined on the same day. August 20, 1798, and both came from America. Whether they were "refugees" from the Declaration of Independence of the former American colonies or whether enough time had passed for the complete acceptance of America as another independent state, it is impossible to say, but Robert Brown is marked as "N. American" and Owen Jones as "America" in the last surviving paybook of the ship.

A woman's body was the first to be washed up. It was weeks before another body came ashore. This time it was that of the Surgeon, William Grey, who was no relation of the Captain. All told only 24 bodies were ever found, one of the last being that of the ship's Lieutenant W.C. Butler, of whose body it was said that it was, apart from damage to his face, in "as perfect a state as if he had only just drowned" – and that was a full three months after the wreck.

The loss of the *Weazle* upset the good citizens of Appledore and their grief appears quite genuine. A full funeral service was held in Bideford and was packed with mourners from miles around. Poems were written:

"The tale is briefly told: – a gallant bark
Embayed, and by the tempest overtaken,
When midnight heavens were glooming pitchy dark,
And wave and shore by the loud storm were shaken,
Drove upon Baggy's horrid Leap – and hark!
The seaman's cry, that never more shall waken
Echo for mirth or woe: – down-down she goes,
And for her fate a long Lament arose".

The Lament, which follows, was well enough preserved locally for it to be published in the North Devon Magazine, *The Cave*, in March, 1824:

HMS WEAZLE

"Lament for the WEAZLE,
The joy of our Bay;
Whose trim was so gallant,
Whose crew were so gay;
Hearts that never knew fear,
Yet confess'd beauty's eye, –
Then rain beauty's tear,
For the day-dream gone by!

Lament for the WEAZLE,
The grace of our POOL;
O! where is her sceptre
Of wide-ocean rule?
The waves in their madness
To freedom awoke,
And the Sea-queen o'erwhelmed
As her sceptre they broke.

Lament for the WEAZLE,
Her voyages are o'er;
She hath made her last port,
She is on her lee-shore;
Low down in the deep,
When the sunbeams are sheen,
And the waters are calm,
May her ruins be seen.

Hope breathed on her sail,
As she went o'er the Bar;
Pride waved in her ensign,
Seen flying from afar;
But her sail it was struck
Ere the Bay she had crost,
Her ensign was lowered –
Her glory was lost.

Tho' the tear fell at parting,
  When love bade adieu,
There was "welcome to ocean!"
  From all her bold CREW,
And the wine-cup was spilt,
  As it circled her deck,
But the blood of the gay
  Is now red on her wreck.

Who hath escaped
  From the tempest's fell sweep,
From the crush of her timbers
  On BAGGY's dark LEAP?
Not a soul: – there was one
  Left behind on the shore,
His fortune to thank,
  But his FRIENDS to deplore.

Comrades in danger,
  Companions in mirth,
Some sleep their last sleep
  In a water berth,
And on whom the tide
  Hath restored as it rose,
By BRAUNTON'S grove-altar
  Is gone to repose.

Lament for the WEAZLE,
  Her voyages are o'er,
From the port she last made
  Came their ship never more:
And tho' memory long
  Our LAMENT will renew,
Fill it up! – but in silence –
  A glass to her CREW!"

The lament for the *Weazle* is extraordinary in that it commemorates the death of quite a small ship by Navy standards. The *Weazle* was one of eight sloops built after 1775. It is difficult to know exactly what to call her, as she was at times referred to as a Brig, a Sloop, and sometimes as a Brigantine. If you want to know what she looked like there is a model of her sister ship,

HMS *Alert* in the Science Museum, London. *Weazle* was 78 feet 11 inch long, and had a beam of 25 feet, tonnage 201. She was built at Sandwich, Kent, and launched on April 18, 1783. She was armed with 12 four-pounder cannon and 16 half-pound swivel guns. She was small, but fast and easily handled, though there was little room or comfort (the headroom between decks being only five feet) for the 106 men who crewed her.

Diving the Weazle

THE NORTH DEVON coast where the grave of the *Weazle* lies is today renowned for its sweeps of clean sand and surfing, but in olden times it was better known as a great trap for sailing ships, so many of which came to grief on this particular piece of coastline that the headland to the North of Woolacombe is still called Morte Point. And Woolacombe Bay itself was named Morte Bay or Death Bay. Baggy Point, on which the *Weazle* perished, is the headland at the southern end of Death Bay. The headland is criss-crossed with paths along which it is said wreckers drove cattle with lanterns tied to their horns to lure ships ashore. You can take that with a pinch of salt, but it is true that Baggy Point was often death point for old-time sailors. The headland is two miles long and half a mile wide, and at their highest point the cliffs plunge 300 feet down to the sea. Baggy Leap is the group of rocks just off the seaward point of the Point. But the *Weazle*, despite the words of the lament, is not there.

The discovery of the true site of HMS *Weazle* was made by the divers of Ilfracombe and North Devon BS-AC, who started to look for her seriously in 1965. In the Winter of 1965 and the early Spring of 1966, the Ilfracombe divers, who included Mr M. Comber, did a great deal of local research into the site of the wreck. They had little success, but a few days before the first snorkel search was due to be made, Mr Comber met an old coastguard who thought he could pinpoint the wreck site. And he could, for just using mask, snorkels and fins, the Ilfracombe divers found a length of chain and one or two copper rivets. The search went on through May and June, and on the fourth organised search three iron cannon were found. At the end of June the weather went wild and stayed bad, so interest waned.

Then in 1967 the branch decided to extend the search into deeper water, but found nothing more of importance. In 1968 one cannon was raised using airbags, and towed into Woolacombe. When the various encrustations had come off, it was found to be in remarkable condition and to have a fine crest. During 1970, one of the Ilfracombe divers, Simon Keeble, was given a grant by the BS-AC to attend a course on nautical archaeology at Alan Bax's school at Fort Bovisand. It was following this course that Keeble and the Ilfracombe divers located the main wreck site some 500 feet in from the actual Point and on the south side of it, and 400 yards further out on the Point from the shore than the sewer outfall, which can be seen clearly.

The site consists of sand-filled gullies littered with kelp-covered boulders, the result of cliff falls over the years. Diving is limited to 40 minutes on an ebb tide. After that the current sweeps all before it out to sea. It is this current that is the cause of deaths by drowning each year among foolhardy holiday-makers who ignore warnings. The sea around Baggy Point is not helped by a strong groundswell. In fact while adjoining bays enjoy flat, calm waters, the Point is often white with foam. The depths vary on the site from two to ten metres, and visibility from less than a metre to eight metres.

Ilfracombe BS-AC was fortunate in its dealings with the Ministry of Defence (Navy), who with great generosity, abandoned the wreck of the *Weazle*, "together with her gear, tackle and accoutrements", to the branch members, provided they signed a form of indemnity absolving the Ministry from any further responsibility for the wreck. This they did. Since then the divers have found copper rivets, two lengths of copper chain (not, it had been thought, generally in use on Navy ships of this period) and some copper sheathing. The recovered cannon was examined by Robert Powers, a local expert, who made some interesting discoveries. First of all, he cleaned the bore and found wadding in a good state of preservation and seemingly made of twisted yarns of hemp. After the wadding came a 4lb ball. Despite 170 years of immersion the ball was completely free within the bore and comparatively untouched by corrosion.

Markings on the cannon identify it without doubt as having been made in the Walker Foundry at Rotherham where the guns for HMS *Victory* were made. It has now been remounted after preservation treatment and can be seen at Rotherham Museum.

There was a report of other cannon being raised shortly after the wreck and taken to Appledore. There is no trace of what happened to them then, and it seems likely that they were reissued to other Naval ships. Another report – in 1860 – tells of seven brass cannon being salvaged from a gully, but local divers believe there are still a number of carriage guns and swivel-guns to be found. Two of the cannon originally found by the Ilfracombe divers are still in position on the site. One lies in a cleft pointing inshore. It rests on some copper sheathing. The other lies in a hole and points up at the surface.

Divers who visit the site today should remember that the *Weazle* remains the property of Ilfracombe BS-AC, and visiting divers are welcome to look but not touch. The remains of the ship are at 51 08 06; 04 15 00W. This is a boat dive. Divers who want to follow the route of the *Weazle* to the wreck site can launch at Appledore into the River Torridge from the ferry slip at Appledore Quay. A concrete slipway is useable for two hours either side of High Water. There is a speed limit of seven knots in the estuary.

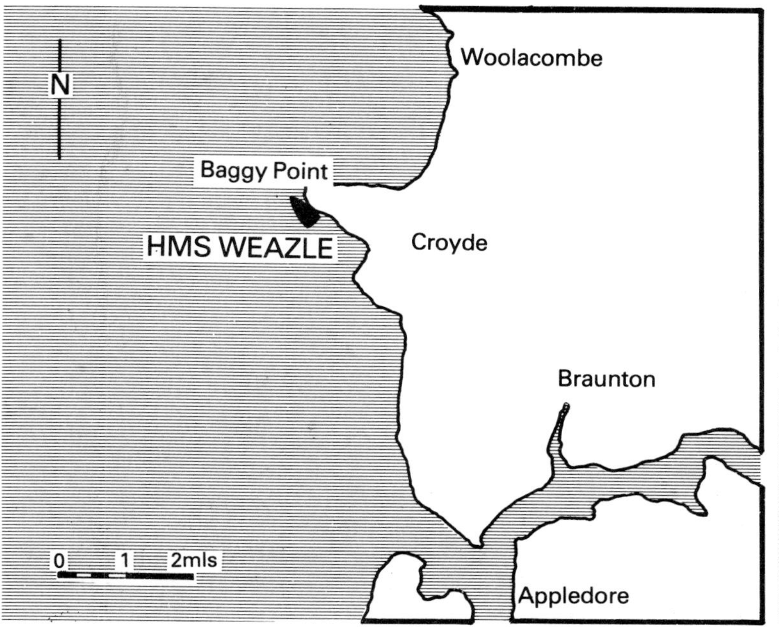

The 'Weazle' lies on sand-filled gullies 500 feet South of Baggy Point.

Weazle wreck log

Position: 51 08 06; 04 15 00W.

Baggy Point, N. Devon

Chart No.: 1164

Date: ....

Dive leader: ....

Equipment used:
ABLJ/STAB .... Air capacity: ....

Suit.. Demand valve ....

Weights: .... SMB/reel ....

Special equipment ....

Dive Boat:...

Weather.......................... Sea Height........... State of tide...........

Current .... Underwater viz ....

Dive timing:
Left surface .... Returned surface..........................

Maximum depth:..

Decompression required..

Seabed type............................ Scour present ....

State of wreckage ....

Area of ship dived: ....

Special points to note: ....

....

....

....

....

....

....

....

....

....

....

MYSTERY OF A WOUNDED WOMAN IN A

The Daily Mirr

CERTIFIED CIRCULATION LARGER THAN THAT OF ANY OTHER DAILY PICTUR

No. 5,058. [illegible] WEDNESDAY, JANUARY 14, 1920 [16 PAGES.]

CLERGYMAN'S RESCUE WORK.

The wreckage-strewn beach on the morning after the wreck.

The Rev. H. M. Piercy, who helped the few survivors ashore.

The coastguard's house at Worth Matravers, where twenty bodies lie awaiting burial.

[illegible] broken in two [illegible] on the rock in Dead Men's Pool.

O[illegible] of the [illegible] of the steamship [illegible], a brand-new boat, which was d[illegible] on the Kimmeridge Rocks, near St. Albans Head, have survived. The Rev. H. M. P[illegible] was up to his neck for an hour in water and shingle, carrying

DEATH BEFORE A

Mr. R. Harris, a Bromley (Kent) rate collector an[illegible] been missing, was found at Felixstowe. A warran[illegible] when a constable called on him, he went into an[illegible] coat. Later he was found fatally wounded, with a[illegible]

LEAGUE OF NATIONS' PR

Viscount Grey, who, it was noticed, was no longe[r] [illegible] glasses, after alighting from the train at Waterloo [illegible] from the States. His name has been mention[ed]

CHAPTER TEN

The Treveal and the Glenmore

THEY SAY IT'S BAD LUCK to change the name of a ship. And they would be right about the ship which changed her name to *Treveal*. Bad luck and disaster clung to her all the days of her short life. She was wrecked on her maiden voyage with 36 of her crew of 43 drowned in their attempts to escape from the stranded ship. But there was no end to the trail of misery even after she was gone. At the inquest on the crew and the later enquiry into her loss, reputations were smashed and careers ruined. The Chief Coastguard concerned was court-martialled, found guilty and dismissed. Even the vicar who had been responsible for saving the seven survivors had hard words said about him locally because of his evidence to the court of enquiry. But after all that died down, the *Treveal* had still not used up all her bad luck. Two years after her sinking a piece of her went like a steel spear into the innards of another ship and dragged her down to join the *Treveal* on the seabed.

The sad story of the *Treveal* begins before they called her that, with the construction of a British standard-pattern cargo ship in the Glasgow yards of Harland and Wolff at Govan. She was designed for wartime use and was called the *War Jonquil*, but by the time she was completed in 1919 the war was over. That was when the Hain Steamship Company of St. Ives renamed her. She became the *Treveal*, a steamer of 5111 tons, 400 feet long with a beam of 52. For her maiden voyage Hain had chartered her to the Brocklebank Line of Liverpool. She sailed from Cardiff in September, 1919, with a cargo of coal for Port Said. From there she was under orders to go on to Calcutta to pick up a cargo of jute and manganese ore before turning home for her final destination, Dundee. On this maiden voyage she was commanded by Captain C. Paynter of St. Ives and 15 others of the 43 crew

Opposite: the 'Daily Mirror' account of the wreck of the 'Treveal'.

were from Cornwall too. Captain Paynter was an experienced captain and seaman and had joined the Hain Company 15 years before.

The voyage back to home waters from India had mostly been a stormy one, and when Captain Paynter reached Portland, he wrote a letter to the owners indicating that he was not entirely happy with the way his ship had handled in the rough seas. Captain Paynter had arrived at Portland at 6 pm on Friday, January 9, 1920, expecting to pick up a pilot for his North Sea trip. He had made the request for such a pilot when he was still coming through the Suez Canal. Now came the *Treveal's* first serious piece of ill fortune. There was no pilot available. At the time this event did not seem very serious. And when Captain Paynter radioed for instructions from the company agent, Collins and Co of Portland, he was told to go ahead without one, and to call at Dover, where he was sure to be able to find a pilot.

The *Treveal* sailed from Portland Harbour at 7.30 pm, and ran almost immediately into bad weather. Some said that the course set then was the course for disaster, and after the court of enquiry months later, an official of the Lloyd's office in Weymouth said that he had watched the course of the *Treveal* when she left harbour and had laid a bet with a colleague that she would run aground. But there are always tales like that after a shipwreck, and in this case the huge storm into which the ship ran was a more likely cause of the tragedy than any wrong course. If you add to the storm the difficulties with the steering about which Captain Paynter wrote to the owners, then you have a real recipe for disaster. One thing is certain: the *Treveal* ran into a massive storm, with giant seas driven by a huge wind from the South-West. Within a short time it was blowing a full gale. Waiting for her hidden under the surface were the Kimmeridge Ledges. Her course now in the rough seas was taking her straight towards them.

It was 15-year-old David Nidd, the youngest of the crew on lookout who saw the danger first. He just had time to shout "Breakers ahead", and then she struck. In seconds she was firmly on to the Kimmeridge Ledges and about a half a mile from shore. It was 9 pm. The seas around St. Alban's Head are bad enough at the best of times, with overfalls on both flood and ebb, but the seas over Kimmeridge Ledges in a full gale is not something any sailor wants to experience at close hand. In the inky black of that January night, the crew thought they would be gone in moments.

But despite the heavy seas crashing against the superstructure, and the roar of the water over the decks, the *Treveal* stood up to all the storm could throw at her, though such a pounding would clearly break her before long. Captain Paynter despite his shock at the strike, immediately put his engines to full astern. Then his radio operator sent not an S.O.S. but a message to the Portland agents, Collins and Co, that they were stranded two miles West of St. Aldhelm's Head (today more often called St. Alban's Head) and required immediate assistance. Moments later the wireless rapped out further details ... "Three holds flooded ... tug required ... urgent". And very urgent it was too. Even though at this stage it seems that Captain Paynter had some hope of getting his ship off, running his engines full astern could not move her.

Now the seas were even bigger, but there was no sign of help.In fact the *Treveal* was in for a long wait for that tug, because she had not even set off yet. The reason for the delay was that Collins' own tug was being repaired. The dockyard tug was on two-hours stand-by, and the crew had gone into Weymouth. They had been called back, but would be some time getting aboard. And it wasn't until midnight that the coastguards at St. Alban's Head were told that a ship was in difficulties. Previously, though they had seen her, they thought she was waiting to pick up a pilot. To them she did not seem to be in any difficulty. This contrasts with the evidence of Collins and Co that they had told the coastguard that a ship was ashore an hour earlier. The confusion was only just beginning.

A moment or two after midnight, William Chape, one of the two coastguards on duty (all the rest were on leave) flashed a message to the ship: "What ship is that?" In reply he received: "S.S. *Treveal*, Calcutta to Dundee, ashore hard and fast. Is there a good landing place?" This was the first indication that the *Treveal's* crew intended to abandon ship – or were considering it. Chape replied: "Yes. Straight inshore. Better wait daylight."

The weather now was worse, if that were possible, and rain had come on the wind, so that the *Treveal* was hard to see, despite the fact that the ship's lights and cargo clusters were all burning. About this time, the *Treveal* wirelessed "Please hurry". But there was no sign of the tug. In the early hours of the morning of Saturday, January 10, Tom Scullard, who was the other coastguard on duty at St. Alban's Head, saw flashing coming from the *Treveal*. With difficulty, and the help of William Chape, he made out the message: "Phone senior Naval officer Portland tug not arrived". The message was phoned through at once, and Portland reported that the dockyard tug had gone out but had failed to find the *Treveal* and had returned to Portland. They would send her out again. The Portland tug, *Petrel*, set out again. At 5.30 am she was in contact with the stricken ship. *Treveal* made: "Are you tug?" Tug: "Yes, what water have you under stern?" *Treveal*: "Heave to. Stand by till weather moderates." Just before 9.30 am Captain Paynter ordered everyone out of the engine room. Then hoisted flag signals to the tug: "I must abandon ship. Stand by to pick up my crew." He emphasised the urgency of his message by firing four maroon rockets at intervals of one minute. At 9.30 am it must have been obvious that the tug could not get close to them. Nor would the Weymouth lifeboat, which arrived too late. And it was clear that the *Treveal* was starting to break in half.

Somehow the crew of the *Treveal* got the port lifeboats launched and into what lee there was next to the ship. Somehow they all got aboard. And then with Captain Paynter in command of one boat, and the Chief Officer of the other, the men hauled desperately for the shore. It seems impossible to believe, but the crew abandoning ship was not seen by either the tug or the coastguards. The wind was at Force Seven, and even in full daylight the visibility in the rain and mist was poor – so poor that the boats heading for shore and rising and falling in the huge waves managed to make the whole journey to the entrance to Chapman's Pool completely unseen. Chapman's Pool is a tiny cove, which though at this time had some fishermen's boats and gear on the Eastern side, is only usable in reasonable weather. In rough seas it is impossible to land a boat anywhere on the beach of shingle fringed with dark shale. As they made the entrance, the *Treveal's* boats made a big mistake. The only decent landing place was by the boatshed on the East, where a channel led through the rocks to the slipway. Seeing the rocks, the boats turned away to the West side and headed for the beach. They were turning away from the only possible chance for them, but did not have time to find out. As they turned they were broadside to the seas, and within seconds both boats were rolled right over by the same wave.

For what happened next we can follow the actions of the man who was to be the hero of the hour, for he told his story of what happened not once but many times, at the inquest, at the Board of Trade court of enquiry, and also to journalists, the most recent interview being in 1969, when Horace Piercy was well over 70. The Reverend Horace Piercy was a young man when he was made curate of the church in the village of Worth Matravers. He had taken Holy Orders after completing his war service in the Royal Army Medical Corps in German East Africa. He was not a strong man, and his physique had been weakened by bouts of malaria during his time in Africa.

The fact that Horace Piercy heard the maroons at all was pure chance. Most people stayed inside in such weather, but Mr. Piercy needed some water, and as the Vicarage well was out of use at the time, he went down to the village pump. While filling his bucket, he heard, above the roar of the gale, a sort of muffled boom. He guessed what it was and took out his watch. Sixty seconds later the noise came again. He needed no more confirmation. Now he knew that a ship was in trouble and firing distress signals. He was a member of the Volunteer Life-saving Detachment, and so made for the village green, which was the detachment rallying place. There was one other man there. Frank Lander, a lobsterpot fisherman who lived in the village, had been mending his gear in a shed next to his cottage when he too heard the boom of a rocket. Lander was also a member of the Life-saving Detachment, and he ran up the lane to get to higher ground to see if there was a flag flying from the Coastguard Station. This flag signal to call out the volunteers had been arranged because there was no telephone line between the Coastguard Station and the village. He couldn't see a flag, but agreed with Mr. Piercy that there must be a ship ashore. "She's probably on the rocks below the Head," said Piercy, and they set off as fast as they could in the direction from which they thought the noise of the rockets had come.

The wind was now nearly Force Ten, and the two men had great difficulty in keeping their feet. To make matters worse, the wind now carried sheets of sleet. However, Lander and Piercy fought their way to a point overlooking Chapman's Pool, and sheltered for a moment behind a stone wall. Looking out to sea was made impossible by the sting of the sleet. It was Lander who had the idea of peeping through the cracks in the dry stone wall behind which they lay, and it was in this way that he first saw the ship. He yelled against the gale to the Reverend Piercy: "There she is – on the Ledge!" Piercy peered through the peephole and saw the ship. She looked to him as though she had broken in half.

Overleaf: watchers on the cliffs see the 'Treveal' break in half.

The two men now scrambled and slithered down the steep track to the Pool. As they drew near to the shore, they saw a scene that

Horace Piercy could never forget. In later years Lander would cry when he thought about it. Twenty-two men had been in the Captain's boat; 21 in that of the Chief Officer. Now Piercy and Lander saw both boats bottom up and all around their keels amid the surf were the heads of men, arms flailing, struggling to keep afloat, choking and drowning before their very eyes. "The men were," said Piercy, "being tossed about like matchsticks." All wore lifebelts, but many lost consciousness almost at once in the icy water. The good swimmers struck out for the beach – two of them, Able Seaman R. Winterbottom and Allan Willcocks, who was the cook, reached it, but there their trouble got worse. Ledges of shale slashed at them and the deep water carved out by waves made a shelf close in. As they struggled up the shingle between waves the loose shingle roared over them and dragged them back. However, in the end both men made it on their own.

In his dramatic evidence to the inquest, William Donald of Swansea, the *Treveal's* Third Officer, told how he had clung to one of the upturned boats. Clinging to the same boat were Chief Engineer Thirkell and the Bosun, but their numbed hands could soon hold on no longer, and they both slid off the boat and went under. Only the Chief Engineer came to the surface again and he struck out for the shore less than 100 yards away. William Donald clung on. But he realised that he was merely being carried by the boat round the pool, and would soon be heading out to sea again. He too let go and swam towards the shore.

Frank Lander and Horace Piercy had now reached the beach, having slid the last part of the track down the ravine. They arrived just in time to see one of the boats lifted up on a wave and smashed to fragments on the shale cliff to the West of the beach. Nearby, struggling in the backwash was Chief Engineer Thirkell. Rolling downwards to the breakers, and nearly finished was the Third Engineer, William Donald. As Frank Lander hauled Thirkell up the beach, Horace Piercy scrambled out over a ledge of rock and got a hold on Donald. Fortunately it was low tide, or there would have no place for anyone to stand on the beach out of the reach of the huge seas. The next big comber washed Piercy off the rock ledge into the sea. But the next wave washed him back together with the man he was trying to save. Frank Lander raced along to them and he and Piercy managed to drag Donald, nearly unconscious, up the beach out of reach of the waves.

The head of another man in a lifebelt then showed in a trough close in, and Piercy went into the sea after him. By forming a very small human chain – just the two of them – they got the man ashore. The Piercy-Lander team succeeded in dragging out three more men. Two of them were completely unconscious, the other was the First Officer, and he was dead. Not that the two men knew that at the time, and worked a long time on the body trying to restart his life. By now they had been joined by more helpers from the village, Monty Hooper and Walter Welsh and their wives. The men helped pull out more bodies, and the women gave artificial respiration. The Cook who had been the first to get ashore, went off his head, crawling into a bush and refusing to allow himself to be helped out, saying that he wished to be left to die. Finally he was dragged out screaming.

When there were no more living creatures to be seen in the sea, Horace Piercy found that they had seven survivors on the beach. The last to be rescued had been a boy apprentice called Kirkby. And he was in such a state that he had to be carried all the way up to the village. By the time the survivors got there, it was nearly noon. No assistance had come from the Coastguards on the Head, and Horace Piercy, who was now, due to his exposure to the icy seas and the wind, in little better shape that the men from the *Treveal*, set out to tell them what had happened. The wind was blowing something close to a hurricane, and Piercy's fight up the path to the Coastguard Station must have been a nightmare, but he later remembered nothing of it. To his amazement when he got there, the Coastguards, despite their watch, had not seen the boats leave the ship. And only now, after the Reverend Piercy had staggered into the station with his news, were the official wheels set in motion. The collection of the bodies started that afternoon.

All Sunday the storm continued, and for most of Monday too. It left a trail of havoc all along the South Coast of England from Land's End to Dover, with coastal rail lines blocked with sand and shingle in great banks across them, chimneys down, roofs off, and much of the West Country flooded. Telephone lines came down too and many districts were completely cut off. On Monday, January 12, the *Daily Mail* carried the first story of the wreck of the *Treveal*, and set the question that all concerned were already asking:

"Of the crew of 43 of the steamship *Treveal* which ran ashore on the Kimmeridge Ledge near St. Alban's Head on Friday night, and which later broke in half, only seven have survived. For 12 hours the 43 waited on the Ledge for the help which never came."

And that was the question: Why had the help not come? Before anything like all the bodies had been found, the inquest opened on Tuesday, January 13, in the little bar parlour of the Square and Compass Inn in Worth Matravers. Mr. Maddock of Wimborne, the Deputy Coronor for East Dorset, was in charge. The press were present in force – they had already re-named Chapman's Pool "Dead Men's Pool" in many papers. There too were witnesses, relatives, men from the Admiralty and from the police, not to mention representatives of the shipping line. As Mr. Maddock opened the inquest in the room which was packed almost to suffocation, there was no doubt that feelings were running high. They were not calmed by the fact that Monty Hooper had rowed out that very morning with his daughter, Floss, to board the wreck. He found the two halves of the *Treveal* about 80 feet apart. Floss, who often went fishing with her father and could handle a boat almost as well as he could, stayed in the boat while her father boarded the bow section. He found it almost undamaged, with the chart room under the bridge intact, the stove in the galley was still warm, and the bread dry in the oven. In the captain's quarters there was room for the whole crew to have taken refuge, and there is no doubt that if they had done so, they would have been alive that day.

Though some blamed the Captain for abandoning ship when he did, it was easy to make such decisions after the event. Captain Paynter had felt and seen his ship breaking up under him, and given the order to abandon her. If the ship had sunk clean away – as it had given every indication of doing – his decision would have been applauded as the only right one. There were other important questions to be asked: Why had the Weymouth lifeboat not been more effective? And on that score two survivors had spoken bitterly of seeing the lifeboat go past the Pool entrance while they were struggling in the water. Why had the tug not found the ship on her first sortie? The Chief Engineer R.H.W. Thirkell of Cardiff declared that if a tug had reached them quickly they could have been towed clear. Why had the *Treveal* sailed without a pilot? Would a pilot have saved them? That question was asked by the inquest jury, but disallowed by the Coronor as "a matter of opinion". Why had the Coastguards not called out the rocket apparatus team and sent them down to the Pool? The foreman of the team stated without any doubt that if they had been on the beach they could have saved many more men with life-lines. And the coroner himself wanted to know why warnings were not sent out to local lifeboats directly it was known that a ship was on shore. The Weymouth boat, for example, was not launched until after 9 am on the Saturday, and the Swanage cox'n was not warned until mid-morning, when the turn of the tide made it impossible for him to reach the wreck. And to be fair to the Weymouth boat, when the men in the water saw her, she was already swamped and unable to turn back to the West in such a wind. She finally made shelter in Poole Harbour.

Anticipating trouble, the Coastguards were represented at the inquest by Mr. Wilkinson, an Admiralty law agent. He said that the situation of the steamer did not become serious until the forenoon. The men at the station were waiting to see the boats leave so as to be sure where they were coming ashore. It was impossible to throw a rocket line over the ship; she was too far off the Head. All of which didn't answer any of the questions, and the Coronor had some damning things to say about stupidity and inertia costing so many precious lives. The jury returned the only verdict they could – accidental drowning. They added a rider commending the gallantry of the Rev Horace Piercy and Mr Frank Lander in rescuing survivors.

Most of the bodies of the crew of the *Treveal* were sent home for burial at the expense of the Hain Steamship Company. Two were buried in Worth Churchyard under a simple cross of Purbeck stone. The cross in the North-East corner of the churchyard bears the words: "Here lie the unidentified bodies of two members of the crew of s.s. *Treveal*, drowned 10th January, 1920 when their ship was wrecked off St. Alban's Head with the loss of 36 lives." The body of Captain Paynter was never found. But even in the burial arrangements, the bad luck of the *Treveal* continued. The offer of the steamship company to send the bodies home for burial came only after an enormous pit had been dug and all the bodies placed in it. Just before the order came to the grave-diggers to take them out again, the sides of the pit fell in, covering the bodies, and they had to be dug out.

Four months later, the Board of Trade enquiry opened in Guildhall at Weymouth. But before that the question about a pilot had been largely answered by a newspaper, the *Southern Times* among its reports of the inquest. The item was headed "The Pilot Question" and read:

"Some misconception seems to have arisen locally in regard to the question of a pilot not being provided the *Treveal*. The whole of the facts do not appear to have come out at the inquest. As is well known in shipping circles, Portland is simply used as a convenient port of call to pick up a pilot, and if one has not been sent the vessel goes out again. Had the *Treveal* applied for a local pilot she could, of course, have had one. But a local pilot would only have seen her clear of the breakwater and headed her on her course."

Certainly the course set was part of the terms of the enquiry. How had a seaman of Captain Paynter's experience come to set such a course? And the enquiry wanted to know too why the message received at Portland about a ship ashore took so long to reach the Divisional Officer of Swanage Coastguard. For it was clear during the investigation that the delay to this message was the reason why the Weymouth lifeboat was not launched in time to reach the steamer before the crew abandoned ship. The enquiry into the loss of the steamer lasted ten days and then the judges announced their findings. They found that the *Treveal* was stranded through an error of navigation. They found further that they could not account for this error "due to the lamentable death of the Master". And in their opinion the heavy loss of life would not have occurred if the Life-Saving Detachment at Worth Matravers had been summoned when the ship first ran on to the Ledges. The Coastguards were gravely censured. They had displayed "lack of energy, efficiency and intelligence." And the court made recommendations for improving the co-ordination between Admiralty, Board of Trade, and civilian life-saving organisations. The matter did not end there. At a Naval court-martial at Portsmouth later that same year, the Chief Officer of the Coastguard at St. Alban's Head, who was responsible for the manning and running of the station, was tried on a charge of neglecting his duty. Chief Officer Frederick Keeley was found guilty, severely reprimanded and dismissed his ship. At the same time the Divisional Officer at Swanage was severely reprimanded for not acting swiftly enough when informed there was a ship ashore.

Even then the trail of misery brought by the *Treveal* was not over. The two halves of the vessel did not break up and sink from sight. For weeks, in fact right throughout the winter, she stayed in position. The ship herself was insured for £100,000, but there was no hope of saving her, or even half of her. The cargo was a different matter. This was insured for £250,000 and salvage started almost at once. Turner Brothers, the Weymouth salvage firm, were given the contract. They started removing the jute from her flooded stern hold. But suddenly the *Treveal* claimed another victim. The wooden drifter they were using to hold the jute was driven onto the wreckage by a rogue sea and then swung off to sink only a 100 yards away. It was a setback, but the salvage work went on. Load after load of jute was saved, even though some was washed out of the hold to litter the shore. Here it proved an additional source of income to the fishermen and other villagers. It was collected, stored and then paid for by the insurance agents.

There were some squabbles over the jute and other wreckage on the shore, with people who came out from Poole and neighbouring areas to take what they could. Nor was that the only thing that troubled the little village of Worth Matravers. They had internal squabbles too. The curate, Horace Piercy, had been very popular in the village with one and all, but after his evidence at the Board of Trade enquiry, when he was asked if the Coastguards could have seen the boats leave the ship, some seemed to turn against him. He remembered his fight against the wind and the way the sleet had stung his eyes so badly and he replied: "Yes, if they *could have* kept their eyes open?". In the report of the proceedings he was quoted as saying: "Yes, if they *had* kept their eyes open". Friends of the Coastguards blamed the curate for the trouble that the Coastguards had got into. It was a long time before the village was itself again. Despite this unpleasantness there is no doubt that Horace Piercy and Frank Lander both fully deserved the award of the Royal Humane Society's Bronze medal which they received shortly afterwards with certificates signed by the Society's president "Edward P." who was later to have a very short reign as Edward VIII.

But that was not to be the end of the *Treveal* disaster. Turner Brothers removed all of the cargo jute that they could find and then started removing her plates and machinery for scrap. To do this they used the tug *Glenmore*, whose Master, Charles Pavey, had been working on the *Treveal* ever since the firm got the contract two years before. On Friday, March 24, 1922, the *Glenmore* left Weymouth Harbour to continue the work. The weather was fine, but when she got right out to sea, a strong South-Westerly breeze sprang up. The wind got stronger and the *Glenmore* ploughed into heavy seas. Those seas drove the *Glenmore* on to the wreckage of the *Treveal*, and a projecting piece of steel spitted her to the stern section. Now there was almost a complete repeat of parts of the *Treveal* disaster. The wind increased from the South-West. Early in the afternoon a message was received at Weymouth from St. Alban's Head Coastguard that the *Glenmore* was in need of assistance. Off went her sister tug *Freewill*, but she couldn't get beyond Worbarrow Bay and had to turn back!

The position on the *Glenmore* was hopeless. The sea poured through the damaged plate in her side, and gained on the pumps. Soon the crew had no choice, and the Master ordered "abandon ship". The eight men launched a boat despite the seas, and headed for the nearest landing spot – Chapman's Pool! This time they made it, and one of the first men to greet them and help them ashore was Monty Hooper, who had been one of the first men on the beach to help the survivors from the *Treveal*! This time things were different. The Chief Officer of St. Alban's Head coastguard station made arrangements for the comfort of the crew. They were temporarily housed at The Square and Compass Inn in Worth Matravers, until a bus came out from Weymouth to pick them up. They were back home between 7 and 8 pm that same night. Meanwhile the *Glenmore*, which was reported to have on board a great deal of valuable diving gear, including new pumps and other lifting gear worth over £1,000, was still pinned to the stern section of the *Treveal*, and when that sank completely out of sight the wreckage of the *Glenmore* went with her.

Diving the Treveal and Glenmore

THE ENTWINED WRECKAGE of the *Treveal* and *Glenmore* is at 50 35 09; 02 04 54W. The wooden wreckage of the drifter has now disappeared.

The real experts on this wreck site are Swindon BS-AC. Proof of this expertise comes if you visit their clubhouse at 37, Dixon Street, Swindon, where strapped to the wall outside the front entrance is the *Treveal's* 1.8 metres long half-tonne anchor. In the clubroom is a brass firehose nozzle from *Treveal*.

The wreck is now well scattered, with large plates lying all over the rocky seabed. Apart from the *Treveal's* boilers there are some parts of her that stand 3-4m above the seabed, but the Winter pounding makes these change year by year.

It is, of course, a boat dive. The main wreckage lies in 10 metres of water, and no wreckage shows above water. It is well covered with kelp, and there is plenty of marine life – notably a nasty conger in one of the boilers. Although much of the wreckage of the two ships is interwined, the two boilers to the North of the main wreckage are those of the *Glenmore*. And though the site has been well-dived, there are still a lot of interesting souvenirs under the plates. Currents are strong and tend to have a swirling action that is funnelled around Chapmans Pool and out again.

Best launch site for inflatables and small boats is at Kimmeridge. The Quay there is part concrete, part cobbles. Cars can reverse trailers down, but launching at Low Water is into very shallow water. Kimmeridge is about two miles by sea from the wreck site. Air supplies from Divers Down on the pier at Swanage; open seven days. Tel: Swanage (0929) 423565.

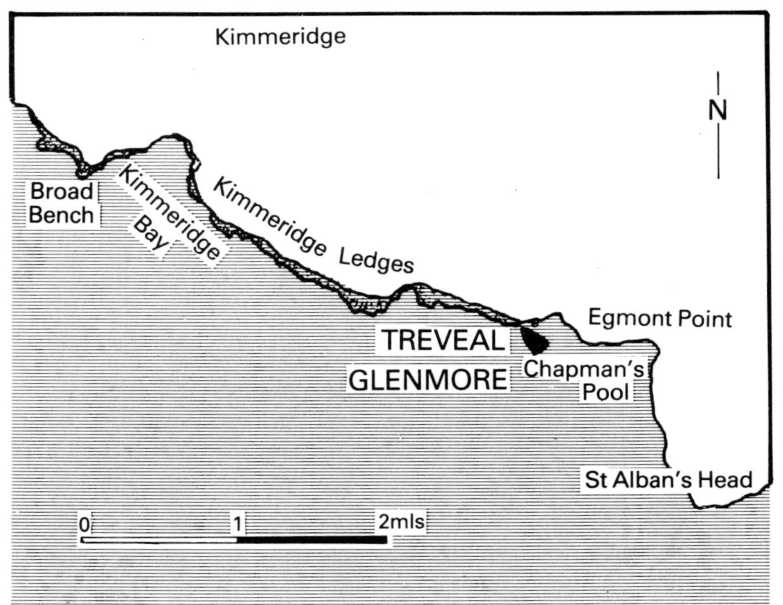

The wreck is well scattered in 10 metres of water.

Treveal, Glenmore wreck log

Position: 50 35 09; 02 04 54W.

Kimmeridge Ledges, Dorset

Chart No.: 2610

Date: ....

Dive leader: ....

Equipment used:
ABLJ/STAB .... Air capacity: ....

Suit .... Demand valve ....

Weights: .... SMB/reel ....

Special equipment ....

Dive Boat: ....

Weather .... Sea Height .... State of tide ....

Current .... Underwater viz ....

Dive timing:
Left surface .... Returned surface ....

Maximum depth: ....

Decompression required ....

Seabed type .... Scour present ....

State of wreckage ....

Area of ship dived: ....

Special points to note: ....

....

CHAPTER ELEVEN

The Lady Meath

IT WAS A HUGE EXPLOSION. So big that it shattered windows in the Anglesey town of Holyhead – two miles away across the harbour – and stunned people in the streets. Above the great breakwater wall of Holyhead Harbour, white water and black debris gouted into the air. When the spray had drifted away it was clear that the *Lady Meath* was not long for the surface. And as for the Royal Navy's nine-ton patrol boat *Manx Lad* which had been tied up alongside the big steamer, of her there was no sign at all. The *Lady Meath* had sailed from neutral Dublin just before midnight on August 15, 1940, and was bound for Birkenhead. But first she had to call at Holyhead for clearance by the Royal Navy Control Service. For while the Battle of Britain was being fought in the skies over South-Eastern England, another battle for Britain was being waged in British ports on the other side of the country. Here, well aware that Hitler intended his U-boats to seal up the entrances to Britain as soon as his undersea fleet could be fully deployed, food and war materials were being landed with all speed. Even so, safety checks had to be made. There was talk of spies being dropped in Southern Ireland by the long-range German bombers who seemed mightily interested too in the British ports which faced the Irish Sea. They had been heard circling nearby in the dead of night.

The checks were made just outside Holyhead Harbour, and so it was that this big British and Irish Line cattle carrier found herself at the tail-end of a queue of ten ships near the South Stack Lighthouse at 5.30 am on August 16. Fussing from one to another of the waiting ships was the Royal Navy's examination ship. The Navy worked fast, and within two hours it was the turn of the *Lady Meath*. At 7.15 am, HMS *Manx Lad* bumped gently against her side and a young Royal Navy lieutenant jumped easily across before the Meath's crew could rig the gangway. Chief Officer Thomas Hodgson led the officer to the bridge where Captain Thomas MacFarlane waited with his ship's papers. The paper work took only a few minutes and then Chief Hodgson led the way back to the gangway which had now been rigged. Seeing him safely across, Captain MacFarlane rang for engines. The officer stepped lightly down to the *Manx Lad's* deck, and at that moment disappeared in a great flash of white light with a red core which was only an instant ahead of a waterspout rising up from the sea.

The explosion seemed right under the bridge on the port side of the *Lady Meath*. And right under the spot where the Navy's patrol boat was lying alongside. The *Manx Lad* disintegrated. The acoustic mine, which had been parachuted down from one of those circling German bombers, had found an important target. For the cargo of the 1597-ton *Lady Meath* was food for Britain in the shape of 700 fat Irish cattle. At that moment not one of the 20 crew, nor the eight drovers on board specially to look after the beef, had time to think of the cattle. The *Meath's* bosun Edward O'Leary, from Arklow, saw the cattle on deck all right, but he was looking down at them for just an instant as he flew through the air, over the ship's rails to land with three broken ribs in the water beside seven survivors of HMS *Manx Lad*.

On the bridge it seemed to Captain MacFarlane that ringing for the engines had caused the explosion – as well it might – but he was stunned and cut by debris. The precautions they had taken to refit parts of the *Lady Meath* before sailing to the war zone from Dublin now seemed a mixed blessing. The interior of the bridge had been lined with heavy concrete slabs for protection against low-level aircrafts' bullets or bomb splinters. This had been standard practice for most merchant ships, following experience gained in the First World War. Then ships had been shelled by U-boats and the bridge had been the main target, causing heavy casualties among ships' officers as well as putting the steering gear out of action. On this occasion though, the precaution had not worked as expected. Though the blocks may well have absorbed some of the blast, some had collapsed, injuring the Captain and trapping Helmsman Jack McGlynn. Depsite his cuts the Captain struggled to move the blocks off McGlynn, and was soon helped by some of the crew, who, seeing the shambles which had once been the bridge, had made for it straight away. Oddly enough, the port lifeboat was totally unharmed, and slid into the water without any trouble. The *Lady Meath's* crew then took to the boats as the ship was sinking fast.

A drifter closed in and picked up the seven men of the crew of the *Manx Lad*, and none of the survivors of the *Meath* were surprised to find that the Navy lieutenant was missing. They *were* surprised to be able to pick up their bosun, who despite his injuries was able to paddle to one of the ship's boats. By 7.40 am the Holyhead Reserve Lifeboat No 647 had been launched and had soon taken Edward O'Leary to the waiting ambulance while a nearby Naval ship picked up the *Meath's* crew from their boats. Much to everyone's surprise and his own, the missing Naval officer was found unharmed, but wet, on yet another ship, and so no human lives were lost in the sinking at all.

Diving the Lady Meath

THE WRECK LIES 1616m on a bearing of 37 degrees from the light on the end of the breakwater, which is the longest breakwater in Britain (1.87 miles). Another way of finding her is to go out to the red channel buoy bearing the word WRECK on it and dive 200m off the buoy to the West. Or even better keep the light on the end of the breakwater and the light on the buoy together and when they marry you are over the wreck. Her position is 53 20 28; 04 36 16. Depth to the seabed is 20-25 metres on high and 15-20 on low. Slack water is three hours before both low and high tides. This is a long period of slack water, but Fred and Brenda Hughes who run the nearby Anglesey Diving Centre and dive the site regularly say you will be better off if you dive when the tide is just picking up a little because it takes away any disturbed silt.

The ship is 350 feet long with a beam of 42 feet, but is fairly broken up. Dave Hudson, a local commercial diver, has been working her salvaging brass and her pumps. He bought the salvage rights from North Staffs Branch of the BS-AC who first owned her many years ago. But there are still large undisturbed sections standing seven to eight metres high from the sand and shingle seabed. The bow section is one of these, and still has an anchor hanging from its chain. Behind the bow is a locker which still has portholes in it. They are very firm.

Fred Hughes, who first dived the *Meath* nearly 20 years ago, is the man to consult about diving her. He often has a buoy on her, so you can make life easy by contacting him at the Anglesey

Diving Centre and School at Trearddur Bay, some three miles from the wreck site. Trearddur Bay is a small holiday village with shops, hotels, holiday cottages and bed and breakfast and caravan and camping places. You'll have no difficulty in spotting the dive centre; just look for the "A" flag. Fred and Brenda Hughes, both BS-AC First Class Divers, can provide accommodation for 30 people in what used to be the Trearddur Bay School, or can arrange rooms in nearby hotels or book self-catering holiday flats for you. An excellent public slipway is within 500 yards of the centre down on to firm sand. Air is available to 4000 psi seven days a week from the dive centre's compressor, and their shop will sell or hire equipment. They will also advise about the closest launching site to the *Lady Meath*, in Holyhead Harbour itself. The centre is BS-AC Recognised School No.13. Tel: Trearddur Bay (0407) 861122 (day); 861053 (evenings).

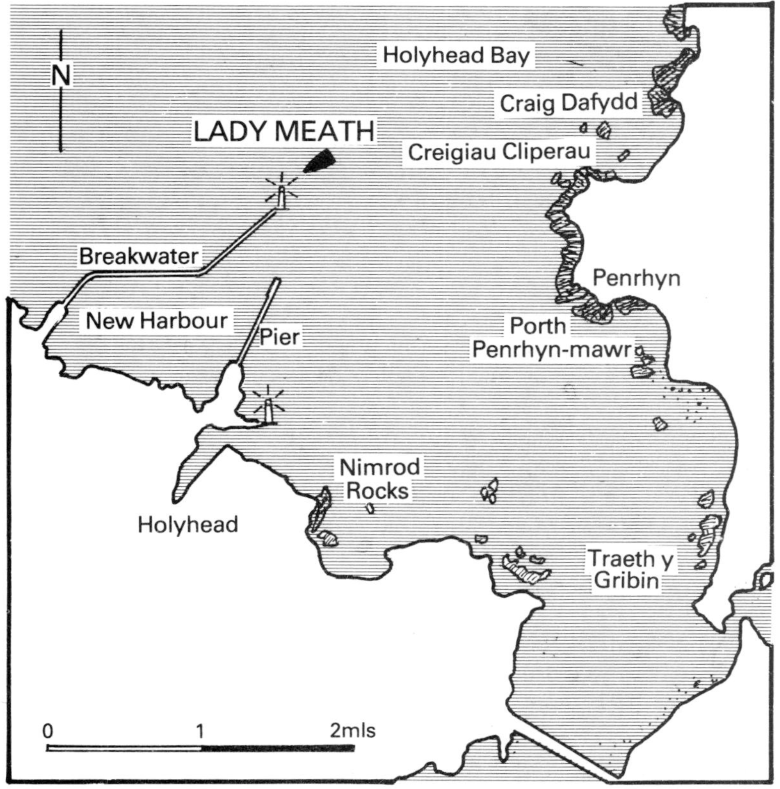

The 'Lady Meath' lies off Holyhead harbour in 15–20 metres of water.

Lady Meath wreck log

Position: 53 20 28; 04 36 16W.

Holyhead, Anglesey

Chart No.: 1413

Date: ....

Dive leader: ....

Equipment used:
ABLJ/STAB .... Air capacity: ....

Suit .... Demand valve ....

Weights: .... SMB/reel ....

Special equipment ....

Dive Boat: ....

Weather .... Sea Height .... State of tide ....

Current .... Underwater viz ....

Dive timing:
Left surface .... Returned surface ....

Maximum depth: ....

Decompression required ....

Seabed type .... Scour present ....

State of wreckage ....

Area of ship dived: ....

Special points to note: ....

....

....

....

....

....

....

....

....

....

....

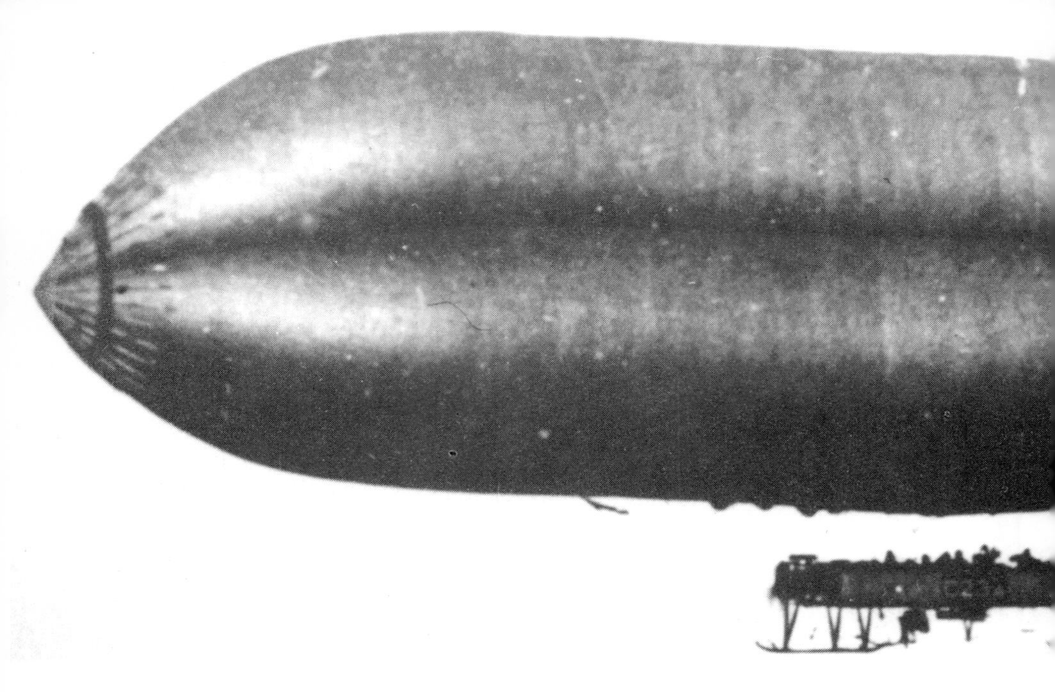

CHAPTER TWELVE

The Shirala

HE WAS SO CLOSE to the little airship that it blotted out the sky. It was so close that Oberleutnant Johann Lohs felt that the hatch cover would scrape on the bottom of the Blimp's gondola. And though he ducked back at once, pulling the hatch cover down on him and yelling "Tauch! Tauch!" all at the same time, he still had time to see one of the British airship's crew heave the bomb by its tail handle outwards as though playing bowls. And he had time too to see the bomb start on a great arc down towards the U-boat's conning tower. The *UB-57's* veteran crew went straight from surfacing drill into a crash-dive routine without any hesitation, but Lohs pulled his head into his shoulders as though the bomb was inside the sub and about to explode on top of him. It was a near thing, for all aboard heard the clang as the bomb struck the casing, but the explosion was delayed, and seemed to

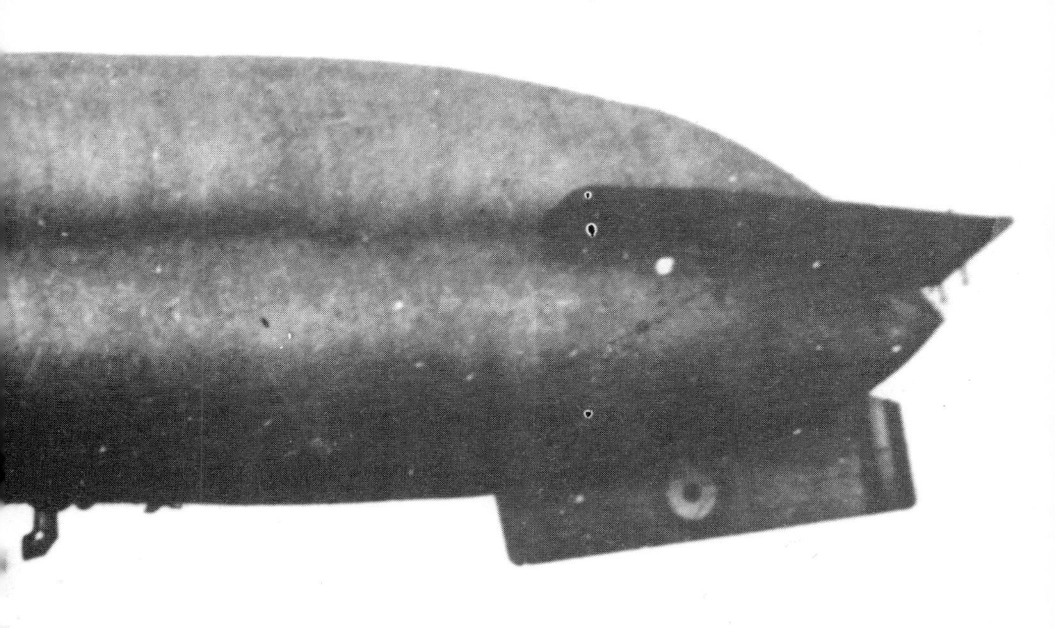

be seconds behind the great porpoise dive of the U-boat. But it was still close enough to make the whole boat shudder and jerk. Lohs knew that they had been very close to death, though he entered the incident in his log quite calmly: "The whole day was spent in this area, and though there was much shipping activity, we were not able to shoot because all ships were strongly escorted and the 'Luftschiff' was overhead."

A World War I 'Blimp' on anti-submarine duty.

The "Luftschiff", or "Blimps" as the Allied sailors nicknamed them, were a comparatively new menace to the U-boats. But by the beginning of 1918 there were nearly 100 of the small airships in service, and aerodromes, airship bases and seaplane stations had sprung up all around the coasts of the British Isles for anti-submarine work. Even so, airships were new to Oberleutnant Johann Lohs, one of Germany's leading U-boat aces, who had carried out mission after mission from the Flanders Flotilla submarine base at Zeebrugge. The first mention of "Luftschiff" comes in his log of the mission he carried out starting on June 27, 1918. By then Lohs had already sunk many ships dived by British amateurs today. It is fair to say that he sunk more ships for amateur divers than any man in history! He personally accounted for over 100,000 tons of Allied shipping, and his "kills" read like a list of today's favourite wreck sites.

Johann Lohs.

In 1918 he sank the *Carlisle Castle* on February 2, eight miles to

the East of the Royal Sovereign lightship, and now she sits upright on the bottom, still laden with the shells and shellcases she was bringing from America. On March 29, he sank the *T. R. Thompson*, loaded with 5600 tons of iron ore, as she was coming up Channel. Seven miles South of Newhaven was the place that *UB-57* found her and sent her to the bottom in 30 metres of water with her bows still pointing to the East. The master and 32 of the crew of this 3538-ton ship went down with her. Only three were saved. The *T. R. Thompson* is regularly dived by boats from Newhaven.

The activities of Lohs and his colleagues of the Flanders Flotilla which had been formed as long ago as March 29, 1915, soon after the German troops captured the area in November, 1914, were a constant threat to the Allied supremacy at sea. Though Germany lost 199 U-boats during the war, the survivors were sinking Allied merchantmen faster than they could be produced, and Britain's food supplies were being strangled by the U-boat blockade. At the beginning of 1918 the torpedoing was so rapid and so serious that something had obviously got to be done about the U-boat menace. Vice-Admiral Sir Roger Keyes was given the task and his plan was to bottle up the German destroyers and U-boats in Bruges by blocking the eight-mile canal which took the German vessels down to the sea at Zeebrugge. On the night of April 22/23, 1918, the Royal Navy struck. Three old cruisers, *Thetis*, *Intrepid* and *Iphigenia*, were stripped of their armament and filled with concrete. They were to sink themselves across the mouth of the canal. At the same moment 200 seamen and 700 Marines launched a diversionary attack on the mole or stone pier at Zeebrugge. They were brought alongside the mole in another old cruiser, the *Vindictive*. While this attack was going on, two out-of-date submarines, filled with explosives, were to jam themselves under the bridge connecting the mole with the shore, and blow themselves up.

Despite great gallantry – eight VCs were awarded – the attack failed. The three blockships failed to reach their positions, and only partially blocked the fairway. The next day four German torpedo boats eased their way around the obstacles, and on April 25, the first U-boat got out too. There is good reason to think that this first blockade runner was *UB-57*. For on April 29, Lohs struck again. This time the steamship *Broderick* was sent to the bottom in 20 metres of water, though her two masts showed at all states of the tide. She had been carrying some livestock, but was really in

Opposite: the attack on the mole at Zeebrugge.

ballast heading for London for a cargo. The wreck of this 4321-ton ship is very broken up, well out off Hastings. The next day it was the *Umba* which sank to the seabed not far away. Ironically the *Umba* was a German war prize formerly called the *Utgard*. She was in ballast and is now broken in half with the highest point of the wreckage coming up to 13.9 metres from the surface. On May 22, Lohs sank the *Red Rose*, a small coaster of 401 tons heading from Littlehampton to LeHavre, though whether he did so with gunfire, torpedo or by boarding her and opening the sea-cocks, he does not record in his war diary. The fact that he knew where she was going suggests that this was no sudden torpedoing, nor is it

likely that *UB-57* would use one of the ten torpedoes she carried on such small fry. For Lohs liked to use his torpedoes to the greatest effect possible. On May 23, Johann Lohs did just that and made the biggest kill of his career. With a single torpedo he destroyed the 9505-ton HMS *Moldavia*, the former P and O liner which became a Royal Navy Armed Merchant Cruiser. And he killed 57 American infantrymen in doing so. For this exploit he was further decorated as the commander of the only U-boat to inflict casualties on the million and more American soldiers who were trooped across the Atlantic after the United States declared war on Germany on April 6, 1917.

Blockships in the canal at Zeebrugge the day after the attack.

On May 26, following his usual pattern during these 10-day missions, he was at his furthest point down Channel before turning for home. The area he favoured for this about-turn was Anvil Point, near Swanage. It was here he found and sank the *Kyarra*. The *Kyarra* was a 6952-ton twin-screw passenger and cargo-carrying liner, which had been fitted out as a casualty clearing ship and on May 24 had sailed from Tilbury for Devonport where she was due to embark about 1000 war-wounded and take them home to Australia. So apart from the crew, six of whom died when Lohs torpedoed her amidships near Durleston Head, there was no one else aboard. The *Kyarra* is, of course, one of the great wreck dives of Dorset. She is in 25m of water and is the property of Kingston Branch of the BS-AC. How to dive her can also be found in Volume One of this series. Once Lohs had seen the *Kyarra* go down, he was off again, up Channel now, putting torpedoes into the *War Panther*, which even so, managed to reach port, and the *Galileo*, which was beached near Dungeness. Finally, *UB-57* slipped safely back to Bruges on June 1.

It was on his very next mission that Johann Lohs in *UB-57* had that first close run-in with an airship. It was not to be his last. On June 27, he slipped out to sea once again, this time from the port of Ostend, which was also connected to Bruges by canal. Lohs did his usual run through all the mine barrages on the surface and once again his luck held. Off Dungeness he wasn't so lucky, for though he torpedoed the 4281-ton steamer *Wilton* and it looked a killing shot, she managed to reach port safely on June 30. On July 2, Lohs was around the Owers Lightship having finally lost the airship, but once again his luck let him down when he hit the *Royal Sceptre* of 3858 tons with a bow shot, but she too escaped and made harbour. A few hours later, however, his luck changed.

Zigzagging down the Channel in full dazzle-paint in the afternoon of that hazy, windless day, came the 5306-ton liner *Shirala*. In this case "liner" didn't mean a cruise liner, but simply a ship belonging to a shipping company which would carry passengers as well as cargo on scheduled routes. The shipping company involved was the British India Steam Navigation Company, who had the *Shirala* built for them in 1901 by A. and J. Inglis of Glasgow. She was 410 feet long with a beam of 50. The *Shirala* started her last voyage – bound for India – on the last day of June, 1918. She left London with her four holds packed with a cargo of wine, crates of Dundee marmalade in stone jars, spares for lorries and Model-T-type cars, including tyres, axles and radiators, telescopes and binoculars. But the main part of her cargo was ammunition for the Indian Army. There were thousands of shells packed in metal crates, thousands of detonating caps, and even some large bombs for aircraft use. And amid this warlike equipment were large quantities of elephant tusks. Taking tusks to India seems like a classic case of coals to Newcastle, but the tusks were in fact African elephant tusks, which were being routed through London to the highly-skilled carving experts of India.

Lohs watched the liner through his periscope for some time. He had made the area around the Owers Lightship his own particular killing ground, and when the *Shirala* was about four miles North-East of the light vessel, he fired one torpedo from his bow tube while still submerged. It struck the *Shirala* on the port side amidships at 5.12 pm. There is some confusion about what happened next. Captain E.G. Murray Dickinson is quite clear in his report to the owners that a few seconds after the torpedo struck there was a second explosion, which carried away the main steampipe and wireless aerials, and put the engines out of action. However, the report of Oberleutnant Johann Lohs does not mention a second torpedo. It seems likely that the second explosion was due to water rushing into the stokehold. As a result of both explosions eight men were killed. But despite the fact that her engine room and stokehold were full of water, the *Shirala* floated for some time, and the survivors who had taken to their boats had time to watch her go down. She was still there when a patrol boat reached the scene and one of her crew had time to take a photograph of the *Shirala* as she sank. Lohs' torpedo must have broken her back, because the ship sank with her still-buoyant bow and stern trying to keep up the deadweight in the centre and she literally folded up in the middle until her forefoot at one end and her propellor at the other both came right up out of the sea. And that is the way she went to the seabed.

Though Oberleutnant Lohs took *UB-57* away from the area as fast as he could, the attack had alerted an airship patrol, and one was soon overhead. Whether this was the same airship which had attacked *UB-57* earlier is not recorded. But the airship now began to follow Lohs wherever he went. The little Submarine Scouting Z-type airships were powered by one 100 hp Green or 110 hp Berliet, or sometimes one 75 hp Rolls-Royce engine. These engines were strong enough to drive the airships along at a fair

Overleaf: dramatic photograph of the sinking 'Shirala' taken by a departing crewman.

speed. But the SSZ's had another advantage. If need be they could hover almost silently over the sea and in shallow water could pick out a submarine's outline quite clearly. And though the bombs were primitive – held by a crewman by the handle at the tail end and then dropped – they were powerful enough to sink a sub when they came really close. However, the airships' real part in the destruction of U-boats was to guide the surface ships to the scene. Most Naval patrol ships now carried highly-efficient depth charges, and when directed by an aircraft or airship, could plant these very effectively. The first U-boat to be destroyed by this air-to-surface co-operation was the *UB-31*, commanded by Oberleutnant of the Reserve, W. Braun. He was depth-charged out of existance on May 2, 1918, when drifters were guided to his position by an airship over the Dover straits.

In *UB-57* Lohs now moved towards the Isle of Wight. After torpedoing the *Huntscraft* of 5113 tons, and killing six of her crew, though she made port safely, he surfaced only to find an airship heading purposefully towards him. The chase was on. It was to make the rest of that mission almost impossible. It certainly got on Lohs' nerves. On July 7 he wrote in his log: "Off Hastings and after a vain attack on a steamer, the airship attacked us throwing bombs down on us. At that went to 30 metres at full thrust and think we rammed an old wreck. Our forepart badly damaged."

However, it was not bad enough to stop them reaching port safely in their turn on the next day. And though he survived the airships and patrols on that mission, *UB-57's* next mission was to be her last. After he had sunk the *Clan Macvey*, the *Glenlee* and the *City of Brisbane*, Lohs turned for home once again. He never made it. On the night of August 14, 1918, all aboard *UB-57* were killed when she ran into a Royal Navy minefield off Zeebrugge.

Diving the Shirala

THE SHIRALA IS A popular dive, and is visited regularly by dive boats out of Littlehampton, Sussex. Her position is 50 40 55; 00 35 10W. Depth is 24 metres. She lies almost North-South, with her bows to the South. During 1978, Metal Recoveries (Newhaven) Limited used explosives to get into the holds, and were reported to have salvaged £150,000-worth of elephant tusks as well as a great number of brass shell-cases. They still own the cargo, and while they have no objection to divers taking a souvenir such as a wine bottle or marmalade jar, they object strongly to the removal of any brass.

The *Shirala's* holds are now open, and the highest point of the stern is about eight metres off the sand seabed. Among the cargo, some of which is widely scattered, can be seen the butts and stocks of rifles, the metal parts of which have completely rusted away leaving just the wood. Somewhere among the wreckage are most of the big brass letters of SHIRALA – a woman diver recently found the big brass "S" of the ship's name.

WARNING: Divers are warned that the bombs in her cargo – some said to be 200-pounders – are lying around the wreck. On a recent dive six were seen on deck amid the debris!

Best centre for diving the *Shirala* is Littlehampton. For details of air and launching sites and dive boats see Chapter Five and HMS *Pine*.

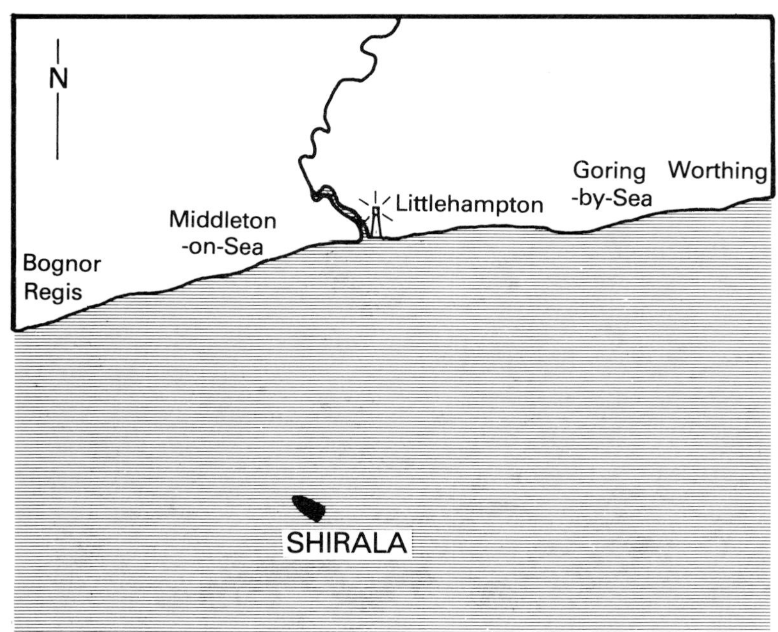

The 'Shirala' lies at 24 metres, with a cargo which includes unexploded bombs.

Shirala wreck log

Position: 50 40 55; 00 35 10W.

Off Littlehampton, Sussex

Chart No.: 1652

Date: ....

Dive leader: ....

Equipment used:
ABLJ/STAB .... Air capacity: ....

Suit .... Demand valve ....

Weights: .... SMB/reel ....

Special equipment ....

Dive Boat: ....

Weather .... Sea Height .... State of tide ....

Current .... Underwater viz ....

Dive timing:
Left surface .... Returned surface ....

Maximum depth: ....

Decompression required ....

Seabed type .... Scour present ....

State of wreckage ....

Area of ship dived: ....

Special points to note: ....

....

....

....

....

....

....

....

....

....

....

CHAPTER THIRTEEN

The Royal Adelaide

MORE PEOPLE DIED in the orgy on the beach than in the wreck itself. That is why the story of her wrecking will not be forgotten, even when the wrecks of bigger ships with greater losses of life have faded into the scrapbooks of history. She was the *Royal Adelaide*, 1320 tons, 235 feet long with a beam of under 40 feet. She was long, slim and made of iron, and when she had all her big sails set, she was fast too. She could run from London to Sydney in a time which made sure there was a handsome profit from the big cargo she could carry. She was built at Bristol in 1865 and was designed for world-wide trading voyages. When she sailed from London in late November, 1872, bound once again for Sydney, Australia, Captain J. Hunter commanded a crew of 31 and had 35 passengers aboard. Below decks she was crammed with 2600 tons of general cargo. Cloth, coffee, cotton, sugar, paper, the very latest in sewing machines, knives, flannel shirts, pins, candles – anything and everything that would find a ready sale in the Australian colony. Stowed in her holds too were hundreds of casks of "Wolff's Aromatic Schnapps", a powerful spirit something akin to Dutch gin. More people were to die from the punch of those gin barrels than were to perish from the crunch of the *Royal Adelaide's* wreck. It is a sad comment on those times that the *Royal Adelaide* will be remembered not for those who died in the boiling surf, but for the debauchery which followed her wrecking.

That she was going to be wrecked was obvious from the early morning of Monday November 25, 1872, when the wind from the South-South-West increased to gale force and the *Royal Adelaide* was sighted from the Portland shore, too close in, and, despite all her tacking backwards and forwards, embayed in West Bay. Unless the wind dropped she was bound to be driven ashore on Chesil Bank. By the late afternoon, thousands of people had come from Portland and Weymouth and miles further around to wait for the inevitable wreck. The *Royal Adelaide's* only chance

Opposite: a mother and baby brought ashore from the 'Adelaide' by rescue line.

Thousands lined the beach as the 'Adelaide' was driven ashore.

was for the wind to drop, but it didn't; it grew even stronger. By nightfall it was estimated that there were nearly 3000 people waiting on Chesil Bank. Mr Hamilton Williams, an eye-witness gave an account of what followed in the *Illustrated London News* of December 7 that year:

"With two companions I set out by the five pm train from Weymouth for the Chesil Beach, hearing that a large ship-rigged vessel had been seen all the afternoon in the bay with apparently small chance of escape. Arriving at Portland, we ascended the Chesil Beach and found the Coastguard in full force, burning blue lights to attract the notice of the ill-fated ship. Presently a blue light flashed from the vessel, whose outline we could just see, blurred and dim through the driving scud. Almost as we came opposite her she drifted broadside on to the beach, despite her anchors which found no holding ground. Fearfully she heaved and rolled in the awful sea. It seemed as if the delivering rocket was never going off on its message of help; but at last straight as an arrow, away it sped right through the rigging."

Once the breeches buoy was rigged, the rescue work got under way, but not before the First Mate, Mr. Powell, was drowned "madly trying to jump unaided" from the ship. Other eye witnesses say that the first man to come ashore didn't wait for the basket. He was a black man who hauled himself hand over hand along the rocket hawser. Next was a woman so fat that it took three men to get her out of the basket. Next ashore was the captain. Only five people were left two hours after she struck, when the ship lurched to seaward, and the mainmast followed the mizzen into the sea. The ship was starting to break up. Those left on board were together on the stern and two climbed into the basket. As they did so the ropes broke and the bodies disappeared into the surf. A married couple and their child were said to be the last aboard. Soon the sea closed over them too. In all six people died in the wrecking. But the orgy which shocked the Victorians was only just about to begin. In the words of an eye-witness:

"When the ship began to break up she opened from stem to stern and presented a wonderful sight of general cargo, just like a huge stores. . . ."

Or, one might say, like a huge bar. For tumbling out of the *Royal Adelaide* on that freezing Monday night came all those casks of Dutch gin. And it didn't take long for all those people to find all that free booze. Men, women and children drank it as though it were water. They staggered about, danced, even made love openly. When they weren't drinking they were looting anything or everything. The orgy went on for three days and nights.

"On Tuesday evening," says one report, "two men were brought into the Victoria Inn completely insensible from the effects of the liquor. One died shortly after his arrival there, while the other was only saved by the opportune arrival of Dr. Rhodes, who succeeded in bringing him round after most persevering efforts ... A boy and a man, both belonging to Weymouth have died from the effects of drink. Other men are but just alive on the beach."

More deaths from excessive drinking occurred on the Wednesday and soon five bodies were waiting for the Coroner. On Thursday a man called Strange, a carpenter from Weymouth, was found dead on the beach from drink and exposure. "Another man named Gilbert, who hawks caps around the town, was also found dead. A man in Bury Street, and an errand-lad, in the employ of Mr Manley, have died from the same cause."

It was not surprising that "Mr. Cotterel of H.M. Customs, seeing the state of several men, smashed cask after cask of liquor so that they should no longer have an opportunity of indulging in their disgusting propensities." In all it is said that 20 people died from drink and exposure after the *Royal Adelaide* wreck. Certainly many more died from her cargo than from her wrecking. Little of the *Royal Adelaide's* other cargo was recovered either, despite ruthless searches by Customs men. Weymouth Museum and Dorchester County Museum today have items from the wreck, which is still there, 120 yards offshore. The gin, I should add, is all gone.

Overleaf: survivors of the wreck, photographed the next day.

Diving the Royal Adelaide

THE WRECK IS AT 50 34 36; 02 28 42W. Approach from Weymouth by taking the A354 Portland Road, and after crossing the bridge over the entrance to the Fleet at Ferry Bridge, continue along the Chesil Beach Road. After 400 yards take the first turning to the right into the large pay-and-display car park, sited at the rear of Chesil Beach itself. Park near the entrance end of this large parking area. Now face the pebble bank, which divides the parking area from the sea. Over on the bank, near its rim and slightly to the right will be seen the old shooting butts. Walk to the rim of the bank to a point roughly 100 yards to the Portland side of the butts. From here look back across Portland Harbour. Approximately 100 yards out from the nearest point of the harbour shoreline, there is a wooden post with a white top. It is easily seen. By walking one way or the other along the crest of the pebble bank, you line up this post with the fort on the southern (right hand) side of the North Ship Channel Entrance on the far side of the harbour. You are now directly opposite the wreck of the *Royal Adelaide*, down the bank and in the sea. Walking distance from the car park to the site is 400 yards.

The wreck is 120 yards out from the shore at a depth of 12 metres. Take note that there are other, different, pieces of wreckage near the *Royal Adelaide* on the pebble bottom. But you can be sure you are on her when you find the huge foredeck winch, which is perched high within the wreck. The whole section which remains intact is the chain locker, lying on its starboard side, with port side and decks eroded away. In calm conditions this site is interesting for the experienced diver and ideal for the beginner. Currents, though, can be moderately strong, especially on Springs, but they run parallel to the shore. Viz can be anything up to 13m.

Warning: Do not attempt to enter the sea if the swell breaking on the beach is much more than three feet in height. In rough conditions getting in is easy; getting out can be downright difficult and dangerous. Any wind above Force 3 from the South or South-West will mean the end of diving here, but an Easterly or North-Easterly, even up to almost gale force will leave the site virtually unaffected.

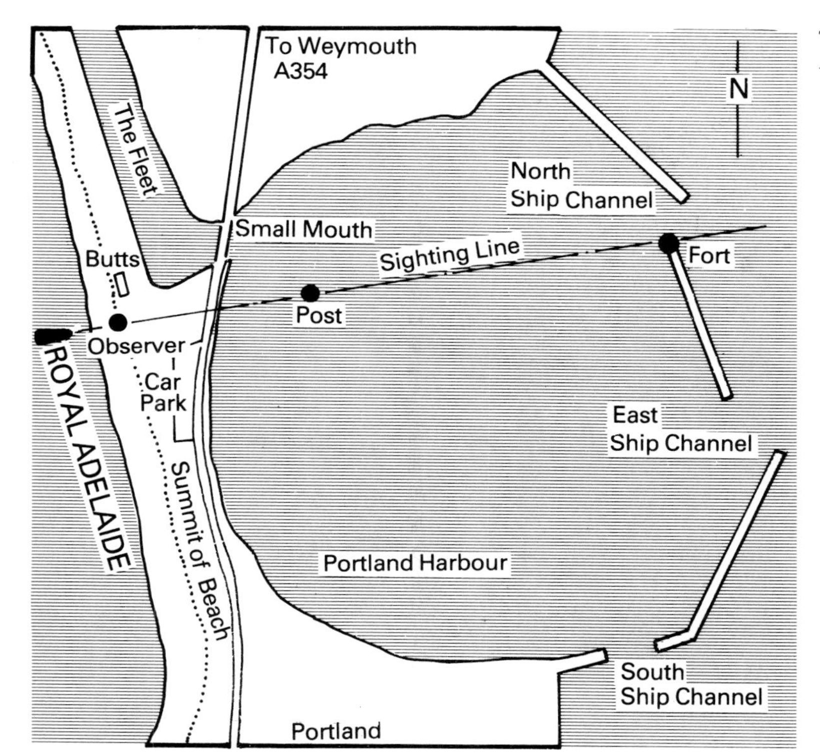

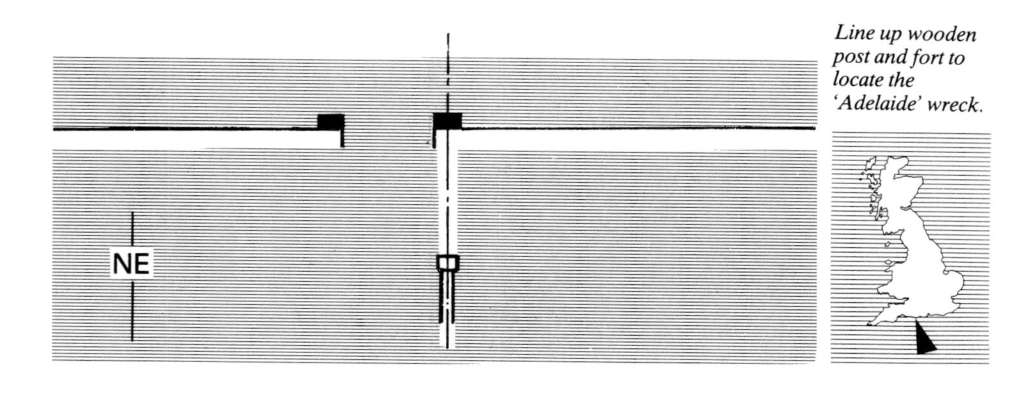

Line up wooden post and fort to locate the 'Adelaide' wreck.

Royal Adelaide wreck log

Position: 50 34 36; 02 28 42W.

Chesil Bank, Dorset

Chart No.: 2615

Date: ....

Dive leader: ....

Equipment used:
ABLJ/STAB .... Air capacity: ....

Suit .... Demand valve ....

Weights: .... SMB/reel ....

Special equipment ....

Dive Boat: ....

Weather .... Sea Height .... State of tide ....

Current .... Underwater viz ....

Dive timing:
Left surface .... Returned surface ....

Maximum depth: ....

Decompression required ....

Seabed type .... Scour present ....

State of wreckage ....

Area of ship dived: ....

Special points to note: ....

....

CHAPTER FOURTEEN

The Loch Shiel

NELSON SAID IT WAS the best natural harbour in the world. One hundred years later a more humble captain prayed to God he could reach it before his ship was overwhelmed by the fury of the storm. Both Nelson and Captain Thomas Davies of the fully-rigged *Loch Shiel*, homeward bound from Australia on January 30, 1894, were thinking of the port of Milford Haven. Captain Davies needed to get into the shelter of the Haven very badly indeed. The gale had struck in the late afternoon and was now turning into a near hurricane. The 1277-ton *Loch Shiel* ran before it with only a few shreds of sail on her great masts to give her steerage. Even so, her iron hull was taking an incredible hammering from the speed with which the wind thrust her into the rising seas. Night clamped down before he could reach shelter, but the Captain knew that at this speed he would soon have to turn in to the harbour or he would end up on St Ann's Head or, failing that, run headlong into Skomer Island.

The *Loch Shiel* nearly made it. She ran in heading for the welcoming shelter of the Dale Roads, but taking too long on the starboard tack smashed straight into the rocks and boulders of Thorn Island. Water flooded in through a great hole in her hull near the keel, and it was clear that her general cargo, which included a load of bricks used as ballast, would never reach its destination. Nor would the Captain and his 25 crewmen bring the *Loch Shiel* back into her home port of Glasgow ever again. She was clearly sinking fast by the stern, and all aboard, including the seven passengers, thought that their last moments had come. But Captain Davies didn't give up. He tried the pumps, but the water gained rapidly in the holds. He ordered the boats lowered, but they were swept away by the giant swell which pounded the island and rushed up the rocks, which sloped steeply up into the darkness. A mattress was brought on deck, soaked in paraffin and set alight. In the wind it roared into flame so brightly that the coastguard on watch at St Ann's Head way across the Haven saw it and telegraphed the lifeboat station at the single-street village of Angle, with its sheltered access to the sea across the sand of West Angle Bay. The boat was launched at once.

On the *Loch Shiel* the situation was desperate. She was held for the moment by the bow, so hard had she smashed on to the rocks, but it was clear that soon the entire 225 feet of her would be under water. The Captain didn't need to issue any "abandon ship" order before most of the crew and a few passengers scrambled over the jib-boom and on to the island. Six other men got into the mizzen rigging and up to the mizzen top. For one of them an invalid passenger, it was a remarkable feat. The lifeboat launch is timed in records as 10.45 pm, and though the *Henry Martin Harvey*, a 37-foot, 12-oared boat, named after the Launceston man whose legacy built her, didn't have far to go, she had a terrible struggle against the gale. Finally, however, the rescue team reached the wreck and prepared to take off the survivors in the rigging. This was done by anchoring and veering down to the almost submerged ship and taking the men off. The invalid passenger was, naturally, the most difficult to rescue, and more than once he looked as though he would lose his hold and fall into the sea. Finally, one of the lifeboat men managed to grab him, and soon all six were in the boat. Then the anchor was taken in, and the boat pulled round to the sheltered side of the island, where the rest of the passengers had taken what shelter they could.

The survivors waved desperately to the lifeboat – and were seen despite the dark – but there was no way that the boat could be brought in over the pinnacles and peaks that speared up out of the water after the passing of each massive wave. It would have seemed prudent to leave the people on the island until full light and hope for calmer seas the next day, but the men in the lifeboat knew from bitter experience that such a course might mean the death of all on the island – only two years earlier in similar circumstances they had been unable to pick up the skipper of another wreck for some hours, and he had died. In fact the secretary of the lifeboat, Colonel R. W. Mirehouse, who was among the crew of the *Henry Martin Harvey* on this occasion, had been there at the earlier tragedy two years before. There was to be no turning back this time. The lifeboat rowed round the island until they found a place where a landing could be made. Though it didn't give direct access to the survivors who could not move from the tiny cove where they were, it did at least mean that the lifeboatmen could get on to the island. That was better than nothing, so Colonel Mirehouse, Edward Ball and Thomas Rees landed with ropes and a lantern. Somehow they scrambled up to a little ledge running along the cliffs and crawled along it, despite the fact that in places it was only inches wide and sections had already fallen to the rocks some 60 feet below. Finally they came to a place above the indentation in which the survivors were huddling. Then it was a matter of lowering the rope and hauling up the 27 people, one by one. The return along the ledge with the survivors was even more hazardous, but finally they all reached the spot where they could board the lifeboat in safety. Huge waves and surf cut down the numbers who could go in the boat. The lifeboat made two trips before all 33 from the *Loch Shiel* were safe in houses in Angle, but by 6.30 on the cold January morning, all the shipwrecked were warm once again.

The following day, as the crew and passengers resumed their broken journey, the *Loch Shiel* was completely out of sight, despite the shallow water. Those shallow, often rough waters prevented the close approach of any salvage ship, so little work was done on her. The RNLI later presented three treasured silver medals to the men who had shuffled along that narrow ledge to save the crew and passengers.

Diving the Loch Shiel

THE REMAINS OF THE *Loch Shiel* are still tight in to the island, in water about six metres deep, which makes it a good, safe dive for novices and snorkellers, weather permitting. Her position is 51 41 47; 05 07 00. The seabed is rocky, with some quite large rocks, but as you go further out from the shore, patches of sand appear. The wreck is covered with heavy kelp growth in the summer. Martin Whittaker and Brian Rogers, of Crawley BS-AC, have been on two expeditions to the area and have some wise advice to offer.

Thorn Island is about the same size as the Mewstone off Bovisand, Plymouth, and the old fort on the top of Thorn Island is now used as a holiday centre for water-sports such as sailing and fishing. Any party of divers wishing to stay on the island must take their own compressor and boats. It would suit divers very well due to the large number of wrecks in the area. Mr Pearson, who runs the Thorn Island Hotel with his wife, can advise on wrecks in the area, and considers the *Loch Shiel* their responsibility. Because of this, Martin Whittaker suggests that any party intending to dive her would do well to land on the island – the landing stage has been built to make it usable at any height of tide – and talk to Mr Pearson, who may well offer them the use of the telephone and bars! A letter in advance might be even better to: Mr and Mrs Pearson, Thorn Island Hotel, Angle, Pembrokeshire, South Wales. Tel Angle (064-684) 225.

Mainland launch site for inflatables is West Angle Bay, which has a nice sandy beach, very suitable for families. Care should be taken when crossing to the island, as the current between mainland and island can reach a considerable number of knots. Crossing takes about ten minutes, and the wreck is a quarter-way round the island from the landing stage at the Southern end near the South-Western tip. Some parts of the wreck, which is of course broken up, are quite large, and timber decking is still all over the bottom, as is her cargo of bricks.

The 'Loch Shiel' is tight in to Thorn Island on a rocky seabed.

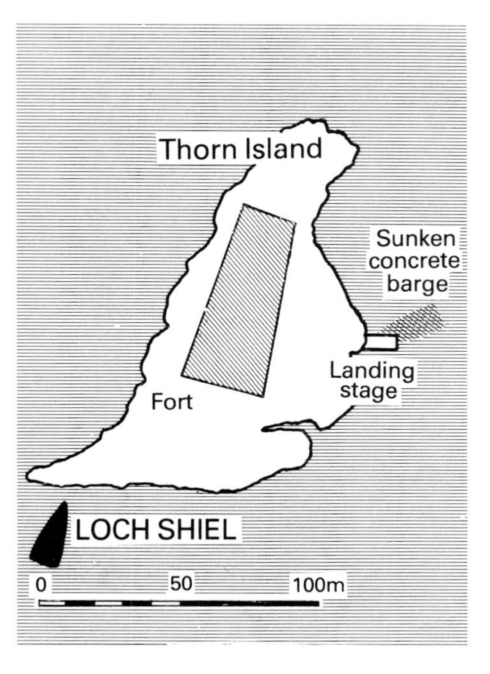

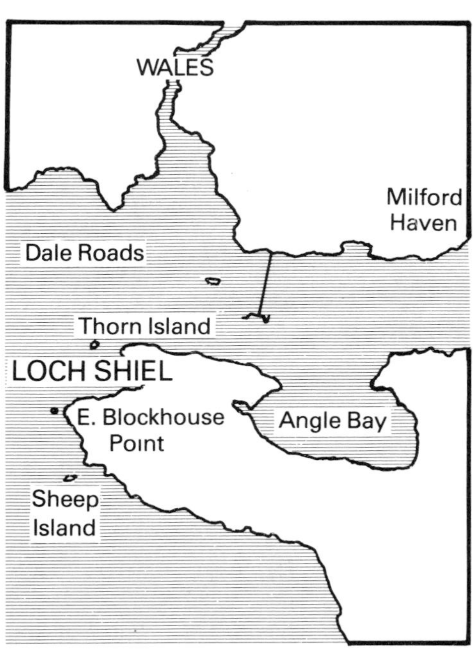

Loch Shiel wreck log

Position: 51 41 47; 05 07 00W.

Thorn Island, Pembrokeshire

Chart No.: 2878

Date: ....

Dive leader: ....

Equipment used:
ABLJ/STAB .... Air capacity: ....

Suit .... Demand valve ....

Weights: .... SMB/reel ....

Special equipment ....

Dive Boat: ....

Weather .... Sea Height .... State of tide ....

Current .... Underwater viz ....

Dive timing:
Left surface .... Returned surface ....

Maximum depth: ....

Decompression required ....

Seabed type .... Scour present ....

State of wreckage ....

Area of ship dived: ....

Special points to note: ....

....

CHAPTER FIFTEEN

HMS Hazard

THE OFFICIAL BIRTHDAY of the Royal Navy Submarine Service is October 2, 1901. This date was chosen for the simple reason that you couldn't have a submarine service until you had a submarine. And the Navy's first submarine wasn't launched until October 1 in that year. Even then you could hardly call the boat very British. Though His Majesty's Submarine No.1 was built by Vickers, she was in fact entirely to the American Holland design, which saved the Navy an enormous amount of research work. This first boat had been laid down in February, 1901, was launched in October, and was on sea trials in early 1902. She was

the first of five boats. There was a great deal of opposition to submarines at first and it is likely that if it had not been for the forceful personality of the man appointed as the first Inspecting Captain of Submarine Boats, Captain Reginald Bacon, and the later enormous support of Admiral Sir John Fisher, better known to one and all as "Jackie" Fisher, the British submarine service would have been well behind that of other nations. Those against submarines denounced them as "dirty playthings". Some Admirals rejected them because there was no deck to walk about on, and the general opinion was that they were hardly ships for gentlemen. The Admiral commanding the Channel Fleet even said that the crews of all submarines captured in wartime should be treated as pirates and hanged!

Even so, Bacon was determined to have a tender or depot ship for his fledgling force, and managed to get command of HMS *Hazard* as a support ship just before the launching of the Navy's first sub. It was something, but hardly ideal. HMS *Hazard* was listed as appointed for "special service", even the word "submarine" was not used. The *Hazard* was out of date. She had

Crew members with an early British submarine (Holland 2) alongside HMS 'Hazard'.

been built in 1894 as a Dryad-class torpedo-gunboat of 1,070 tons, and carried two 4.7-inch and four 3-pounder guns as well as her five torpedo tubes. Her crew numbered 120. She joined the Submarine Service at Barrow in Furness, where the Holland boats were being built in the yards of Vickers and Maxim Ltd. The first of them was built with great secrecy in a shed which was said to be housing a special kind of pontoon. Her launching was secret too. There was no ceremony, and soon after the Navy took delivery of her, the Americans sent over a crew to teach the members of the new submarine service how to handle their first boat. But the exchange of skills was not all one-sided. During the early trials Captain Bacon hit on the idea of fitting a periscope, and the first "optical tube" was fitted. The Americans took the idea back to the States with them.

HM Submarine No.1 was designed to do 8 knots on the surface and 7 knots submerged. To get under took from two minutes to 10 minutes "dependent on the skill of the crew", and her maximum safe depth was listed as 100 feet. The time she could stay submerged was said to be three hours. It was in tests of this last specification that *Hazard* played her first recorded role in looking after her submarines. Commander Richard Compton-Hall, who is the Director of the Royal Navy's Submarine Museum, and commanded submarines himself, tells in his book *Submarine Boats* how Captain Bacon tested out this underwater endurance time with a series of "fug trials", with the tiny breadroom of HMS *Hazard* standing in for the cramped quarters of the Holland boats. To start with, four men were shut in the breadroom for two and a half hours without any ill effects from carbon dioxide which rose to 9.5 parts per thousand. Bacon himself took part in later tests. "Tests in the breadroom were uneventful: the subjects passed the time with cards and music; and every hour the doctor took everyone's pulse and temperature including his own. Something serious was expected to happen, and the medical experts were disappointed when nobody collapsed."

The tests were then transferred to the actual submarine, and even when two complete crews were shut inside for a whole night, there were no breathing difficulties for any of them. But they had to endure something worse. An elderly representative of the Holland Company brought his flute along to entertain the company, but as is usual with amateur entertainers with a captive audience, overdid it and played all night long. Captain Bacon is recorded as saying that every man concerned "looked upon flutes afterwards with a personal measure of animosity".

The first submarine nearly sank *Hazard* when out for one of its first surface runs. Something went wrong with the steering, and she rammed her depot ship so hard that her bows penetrated right through to the sick bay, to the great alarm of those who were in there in the berths. Holland 1 made her first dive on Good Friday, March 20, 1902.

In the summer of 1902, the complete Royal Navy Submarine Service sailed down to Portsmouth. This move actually involved *Hazard* and two submarines – all that were operational. The three others joined them later. Now serious sea training started in the Solent. The submarines were still disapproved of in many quarters, and so tended to keep themselves to themselves. Soon they were accused of being a private navy. Certainly they were a tight little group of men who lived, talked and breathed submarines. But their one big advantage was the patronage of Admiral "Jackie Fisher". Fisher may have been over 60, but he was no fool, and more importantly in his drive to modernise the Navy, he had the ear of the King. Into the Royal ear he dropped every piece of good news he could about the submarine service, and particularly about their success if manœuvres in "sinking" the great ships of the men who opposed their use. When the "A" Class came into service with the Navy, "Jackie" Fisher managed to get the King to give permission for the Prince of Wales (later George V) to go for a dive in the first one. Such a Royal event would these days, of course, have received huge publicity with pictures in all the papers, but even if in those days the publicity was not so great and mostly for internal consumption, it must have got the message over to those who were still against the Navy having submarines: these infernal weapons were here to stay.

There was another lobby against the Heir to the Throne going on this voyage in HMS *A-1* – and this was from those who opposed it on grounds of safety. When the trip actually took place everyone appeared terribly confident, and the Princess of Wales on the deck of *Hazard* remarked with a smile that she would "be very disappointed if George doesn't come up again" and everyone including "Jackie" Fisher laughed dutifully. Later Fisher was to say that he "was jolly glad" when the Prince reappeared after the dive in the Solent. It was too a great demonstration of Royal approval of the Navy's submarine service. It could easily have gone wrong. How easily was shown only a few days later when *A-1* became Britain's first submarine service loss. She was sunk by accident during manœuvres in the solent when she was aiming to let off a dummy torpedo at the cruiser *Juno*. Her commander was just lining up to fire when he was run down by the Castle Line steamer *Berwick Castle* on her way from Southampton to Hamburg. The Captain of the *Berwick Castle* saw the little submarine at the last moment, and though he ordered his engines to full astern at once and put his helm hard to starboard, he struck the sub a shattering blow, and she plunged straight to the seabed with the loss of her 11 crew.

It was a disaster, but "Jackie" Fisher didn't waver in his support of the submarine as a vital weapon for any future war. In fact he forecast pretty accurately what would happen in the Great War which was still nearly ten years ahead when he wrote in a letter dated April 20, 1904: "In all seriousness I don't think it is even faintly realised – the immense impending revolution which the submarines will effect as offensive weapons of war. When you calmly sit down and work out what will happen in the narrow waters of the Channel and the Mediterranean – how totally the submarines will alter the effect of Gibraltar, Port Said, and Malta, it makes one's hair stand on end!" He was right, of course, and gradually the Navy moved towards thinking that the submarine could be of use in a war, though some still thought in hunting, shooting and fishing terms and believed the best use of submarines would be to tow the submarines over to an enemy port and then put them in "like ferrets to flush 'em out" when presumably both fleets would then do battle like real gentlemen on the surface!

The "A" Class now in service cost £41,000 each, and the "B" and "C" Classes followed swiftly, even if more expensive at £47,000 each. But they were still driven by petrol engines. Though one British boat, the *A-13*, was fitted with diesel engines by 1905, it was not until 1908 that the first of the "D" Class was launched, complete with diesel engines. Many people think that at this time in the development of submarines the Germans were well ahead of us, but it is not so. Though Herr Rudolf Diesel was of course a German, and the engine bears his name, the diesel engine principle of compression-ignition was first patented by one Herbert Akroyd Stuart, an English engineer in 1890. Herr Diesel however improved the engine so much that it was given his name in 1893. Before the launching of *U-19*, German submarine engines were powered by paraffin. Both nations of course used electric motors underwater.

During all this time HMS *Hazard* was a familiar sight in the Solent area and in the Channel itself, at first with her brood of stubby 63-foot Holland boats around her. Then she was home to many "A" Class submarine crews with bigger boats of 100 feet long and more, and more came to know her well as the training of crews increased and the scent of war grew stronger every year. The arrival of the "D" Class meant that the boats around the *Hazard* were now much, much larger. The "D" Class of 1908 were for example 164 foot 7 inches long and of 495 tons. And the "E" Class of 1911 was 30 feet longer than that, with a safe diving depth now of 200 feet. Her speed on the surface was 14 knots and she could do over 9 knots submerged. She had two 18-inch bow tubes, one stern tube and two 18-inch beam tubes, a 12-pounder gun and could carry 10 torpedoes. Fifty-six of these boats were to be built. But the *Hazard* was still home to the Navy's Submarine Service – and "The Trade" as they call it grew very used to the old ship with her crest of a silver die or dice on a field of green, and her motto "*Facta est alea*" (The die is cast).

The die was well and truly cast on August 4, 1914 when war was declared. The slow work up to the war had cost the Submarine Service dear. *A-1* and *C-11* were sunk by ramming. Battery and gas explosions in other submarines caused many more casualties. *A-8* sank in Plymouth Sound in 1905 when her captain drove her too fast on the surface, and she put her nose under with the hatch still open. The loss of *A-3* was a particularly terrible tragedy. For the submarine was struck by *Hazard* herself on February 2, 1912, when taking part in exercises in the Solent. The Germans seem to have suffered less in their submarine development than other nations – only one U-boat was lost before the war, and that was the *U-3* on January 17, 1911, but she was salvaged and put back to work later.

At the start of the 1914-18 War, there is no doubt which nation had the edge in the number of submarines available. The Royal Navy had 70 ready or just about ready for use. Germany had 30. And if this looks as though the Royal Navy could run rings round the opposition, it must be said that the Navy's world-wide commitments had so widely dispersed their submarines all over the world that there were not all that many available in home waters to deal with the Kaiser's great fleet. Now *Hazard* was not alone in looking after the submarines. HMS *Thames, Maidstone, Adamant* and *Alecto* joined in the mothering.

The submarine war started slowly for the Navy with a dawn

'Hazard' with three submarines alongside: a picture postcard of 1908.

patrol on August 5 by *E-6* and *E-8* from Harwich to carry out a recce of the Heligoland Bight. They found no targets. And first blood was to go the Royal Navy's surface ships, even though *U-15* made the first torpedo attack of the war on August 8 against HMS *Monarch*, which was carrying out a practice shoot with others near Fair Isle. The torpedo missed, but was close enough for the lookouts on the British battleship to see its white trail. *U-15* submerged, but clung on to the battle group. She was spotted again by both the battleships *Dreadnought* and *Iron Duke*, but when they tried to ram her, she got away again. The next morning *U-15's* engines broke down, she was spotted by the light cruiser HMS *Birmingham* on the surface, and some of the Navy men heard hammering coming from the submarine as though repairs were being carried out. The *Birmingham* didn't hesitate. She swung round and rammed. Her bows caught the submarine a glancing blow and the *U-15's* number could be seen quite clearly painted on her bow which was pushed up by the strike. But for some reason she stayed on the surface and the cruiser had time to come round again in a tight circle and this time hit her square on. *U-15* was clean in half just in front of the conning tower and the two halves floated for several minutes before sinking. There was no sign of her crew.

The score was evened not long afterwards when Kapitanleutnant Otto Hersing in *U-21* sank the light cruiser HMS

Pathfinder and sent her to the bottom of the Firth of Forth. Hersing had sunk the first ship to be destroyed by a submarine since the American Civil War! The Royal Navy's Submarine Service scored its first victim when Lieutenant-Commander Max Horton in *E-9* sank the German cruiser *Hela* on September 13. And then the submarine war was well and truly on. The Royal Navy's submarines were highly successful, and so were the German U-boats. One tends to hear more about the U-boats because they were operating in the North Sea and English Channel, whereas the British boats were often scoring all their successes far away overseas.

During next three years of war *Hazard* was very prominent, but acting more as a tender than a mother ship. She was carrying out that role when the end came for her on January 28, 1918. It came not from mine or torpedo but from the steamer *Western Australia* which suddenly loomed up out of the murk on that January evening square on her port bow. The *Hazard* was looking after the submarines of the Fifth Submarine Flotilla in the Solent, though the flotilla was normally based at Dover. The *Western Australia* of 2937 tons was a casualty clearing vessel, but was also described as an ambulance ship, and regularly carried casualties home from the trench warfare in France. She carried a stern-mounted 4.7-inch defensive gun and was more than twice the size of *Hazard*. She sliced into the side of the aged support ship, cutting her almost clean in half. *Hazard* sank like a stone. So quickly in fact that it is surprising that only three men were drowned. But another died later from the injuries he received as the big steamship struck. All the rest of *Hazard's* crew were picked up by the ship which sank them. But it was still wartime and though censorship had been slightly relaxed, the Secretary of the Admiralty was not giving anything away when he allowed this terse statement to appear on Page Seven of *The Times* of January 30, 1918:

"HMS *Hazard*, torpedo-gunboat, was sunk in the English Channel on January 28 as the result of a collision. Three men were lost. All the next-of-kin have been informed."

Later editions of *The Times* carried the following:

"The Secretary of the Admiralty announces the following casualties. HMS *Hazard*. Drowned. Brown H.G. Shipwright 1st Class 346243 P.O.; Primmer, W.Sto.P.O. 299650 Po; Rendle P.W. Sto. 2nd Class K 40297. Died of Injuries. Abbey, A.F. Ldg Carp. Crew M. 8249 Po."

Such a short wartime announcement was nothing new. There had been many others like it during the three years of war that had already past. The Secretary of the Admiralty was very conscious that the Germans seemed very well informed about our shipping losses. In fact U-boat commanders wrote the names of their victims in their war logs with no apparent hesitation immediately on their return from a mission. So the Admiralty was not giving anything away – even when the loss was as the result of a collision. In *Hazard's* case his hesitation to give more than the bare facts was probably understandable, though it is doubtful if the German Navy were taken in by the description of the ship as a "torpedo-gunboat". They must have known that HMS *Hazard* was in fact Britain's first submarine depot ship.

Diving HMS Hazard

HMS HAZARD, WHICH WAS 250 feet long with a beam of 30, lies at 50 43 45; 01 03 14W in 22 metres near the Solent Warner Shoal Buoy and some two miles off Bembridge in the Isle of Wight. Two miles away from her is Britain's first submarine service loss, the *A-1*. Divers should check whether the *Hazard* has been designated as a war grave before diving this one. And they should take great care when doing so. The wreck lies North-South just half-a-mile East of the Warner Buoy, and is in the centre of the deepwater channel leading into the Eastern Solent. This is an extremely busy area with many ferries, tankers and Naval ships on the move most of the time.

It is a dive for the very experienced only and with maximum cover required. Visibility is usually not good, and tides can be very strong. The *Hazard* is almost completely upside down and well sunk into the soft black mud of the seabed. Her bronze props were salvaged some years ago. Due to the boat traffic in the area this should be a hard-boat dive with an experienced skipper, and his advice should be sought before diving. Such a man is Martin Pritchard, 46, Bellecroft Drive, Newport, Isle of Wight PO30 2JH. Tel: 0983-525169. His 27-foot dive boat *Explorer* for 10 divers is based in Bembridge. He can also supply air.

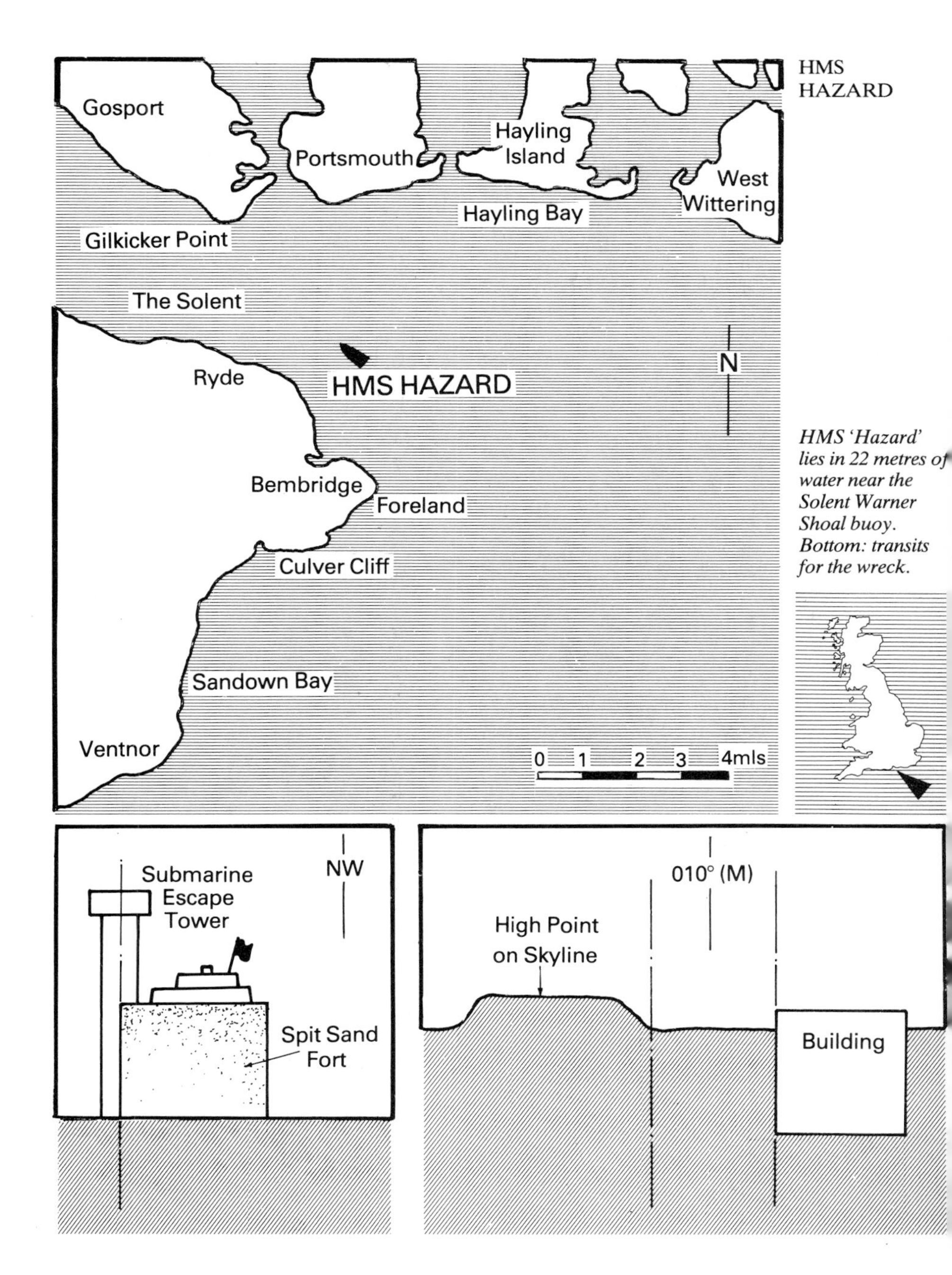

HMS 'Hazard' lies in 22 metres of water near the Solent Warner Shoal buoy. Bottom: transits for the wreck.

Hazard wreck log

Position: 50 43 45; 01 03 14W.

Off Bembridge, Isle of Wight, Hants.

Chart No.: 2045

Date: ....

Dive leader: ....

Equipment used:
ABLJ/STAB .... Air capacity: ....

Suit .... Demand valve ....

Weights: .... SMB/reel ....

Special equipment ....

Dive Boat: ....

Weather .... Sea Height .... State of tide ....

Current .... Underwater viz ....

Dive timing:
Left surface .... Returned surface ....

Maximum depth: ....

Decompression required ....

Seabed type .... Scour present ....

State of wreckage ....

Area of ship dived: ....

Special points to note: ....

....

Index

PICTURE CREDITS: Ted Shipsey (front and back covers, p. 82); Rex Cowan (frontispiece, 30, 42, 76); Imperial War Museum (10, 48, 60, 100, 148, 152); RAF Coltishall (21, 22, 24, 26); Alan Bax (43); Dartington Rural Archive (54); Public Record Office (62, 66); National Maritime Museum (78); Newhaven Historical Society (80); Hay Wrightson (103); The Science Museum (114); Syndication International (124); Illustrated London News Picture Library (150, 162); Dorset County Library (130, 164); A.E. Cocksedge (166); Royal Navy Submarine Museum (180, 184).